UNDER THE RED ENSIGN
BRITISH PASSENGER LINERS
OF THE '50s & '60s

10/19 RAM

RAM

Cunard

UNDER THE RED ENSIGN

BRITISH PASSENGER LINERS
OF THE '50s & '60s

WILLIAM H. MILLER

The
History
Press

For Commodore Ronald Warwick and his wife Kim,
both of whom have given so many wonderful shipboard moments

Front and back cover images by Stephen Card.

Frontispiece: A classic Cunard menu cover from the
Mauretania in the 1950s.

First published 2008

The History Press Ltd
The Mill, Brimscombe Port
Stroud, Gloucestershire, GL5 2QG
www.thehistorypress.co.uk

Reprinted 2009

British Library Cataloguing in Publication Data.
A catalogue record for this book is available from the British Library.

ISBN 978 0 7524 4619 6

Typesetting and origination by The History Press Ltd.
Printed in Great Britain

CONTENTS

FOREWORD

Like thousands of others, tens of thousands in fact, I went to sea in the late 1950s. Then, in Britain, a career in the merchant service offered great opportunity. Alone, there was the attraction of travel, visiting places and far-off lands that one had only read about. There was that great sense of adventure blended with steady employment, perhaps a long career if one wanted it. I was quite lucky. My first ship was the almost brand new *Reina Del Mar* of Pacific Steam Navigation. With her white hull and yellow funnel and three classes of passengers, plus space for lots of freight, she'd leave Liverpool and head across the mid-Atlantic to the Caribbean, to the likes of Havana, Trinidad and Curacao, then pass through the Panama Canal and visit ports along the West Coast of South America as far south as Valparaiso. A full voyage back to Liverpool took seventy days. I was then a 'boy cook', working in the lower-deck kitchens, which were on water level and so quite low enough. I earned £9 a month. But like so many others, I later made my way around to Liverpool waterfront, seeking work aboard other ships with the then numerous British shipping companies. Eventually, I joined the great Cunard Line and sailed on the North Atlantic on such ships as the *Britannic*, then the last of the White Star Line, and the *Parthia*, a combination ship that carried only 250 passengers plus lots of cargo. I also spent time on the *Queens*, the famous *Mary* and *Elizabeth*, and cruising the world onboard the Green Goddess, the legendary *Caronia*. We sailed to New York and I well remember the long stays at Piers 90 and 92, enjoying that incredible city and walking to places like Broadway, Times Square and Fifth Avenue. Later, I joined Royal Mail Lines and, as chief larder cook, served aboard the splendid *Andes*, then one of the finest cruise ships afloat. Now, my voyages were very varied – cruising to ports such as Naples and Haifa, Dakar and Freetown, Rio and Barbados.

But then and like many others, I later left the ships and went to work ashore. I would sail again, however, in 1975, but never again on liners and instead aboard Australian cargo ships as chief cook. Of course, that was quite different.

Having met in Bermuda in 1970, Bill Miller and I have been friends for over thirty-five years and together we have discussed the great British passenger ships of the 1950s and '60s, those bygone liners from a different age. In this, his latest book, those ships come alive again – in photos, histories, recollections and anecdotes from passengers as well as staff. It is a great tribute to those fine liners, ones that once were so familiar, such a part of British life and which lined the docks at Southampton, London and, close to my home, at Liverpool. I for one am indebted to Bill for creating yet another deeply nostalgic look, a grand review in fact, of those great British passenger ships, from Anchor Line to Union Castle. Once again, I can almost see, say, the *Reina Del Mar* in the Mersey!

Robert Welding
Wollongong, Australia
Summer 2008

ACKNOWLEDGEMENTS

It takes nothing short of a full crew to muster a book such as this of maritime histories, anecdotes and recollections, and of course the photographs. I am deeply indebted to all. I am merely the chief purser of sorts, sorting and organizing the material – and then, perhaps, becoming the marine architect in arranging the format of the book. Mostly, it is a work of complete joy and thorough reward. The mission has a singular purpose: documenting these bygone passenger ships and maintaining (and perhaps enhancing) their heritage. Of course, there are the ships' personnel, the office staffs, the passengers and even perhaps the dockers, the provisions and fuel oil crews, and those from the shipyards that built them and later repaired and refitted them. Overall, it is a rich collection of passenger ships, almost like none other anywhere else.

First, I must thank The History Press for taking on this work; they do a splendid job in book production. Then there are two dear friends: Stephen Card for his wonderful covers and Robert Welding for his evocative foreword. Great appreciation goes to my 'loyalist' crew – Frank O. Braynard, Tom Cassidy, Anthony Cooke, Luis Miguel Correia, Richard Faber and Michael Hadgis. And, of course, enormous praises to Abe Michaelson, who has helped me in many ways with these liner books for some twenty-five years.

Kind appreciation to other 'crewmembers' – Hans Andresen, the late Frank Andrews, Scott Baty, Anne Beckwith-Wallace, Joan Benton-Smith, Ian Boyle, John Butt, Peter Buttfield, J.K. Byass, Michael Cassar, Bernard Chabot, John Crabb, the late Frank Cronican, Bill Deibert, John Dimmock, John Draffin, the late Alex Duncan, John Ferguson, Yoshiatshu Fukawa, the late John Gillespie, Brian Gregory, John Havers, Stanley Haviland, Desmond Kirkpatrick, Peter Knego, Clive Harvey, Andy Hernandez, Charles Howland, the late F. Leonard Jackson, Brenton Jenkins, Norman Knebel, Alex and Mhairi Lang, John McFarland, Captain James McNamara, the late Vincent Messina, the late Dean Miller, James Moran, Richard Morse, Ian Noble, Hisashi Noma, Robert Pabst, Mario Pulice, the late S.W. Rawlings, Gemma Richardson, Fred Rodriguez, Ray Rouse, David Rulon, Captain Terry Russell, Selim San, Captain Dennis Scott-Mason, the late Antonio Scrimali, James L. Shaw, Roger Sherlock, Tony Slaven, Captain Harvey Smith, John Smythe, the late C.M. Squarey, Captain Ian Taylor, the late Everett Viez, Commodore and Mrs Ronald Warwick, Steffen Weirauch, Albert Wilhelmi and Victor Young.

Companies and other organisations that have assisted include Canadian Pacific Steamships, Crystal Cruises, Cunard Line, Ellerman Lines, P&O, Port Authority of New York & New Jersey, Steamship Historical Society of America and the World Ship Society.

INTRODUCTION

The Port of London was once the shipping capital of the world. Over 100 large ships could be at the seemingly endless docks at any one time. Special sightseeing cruises were run just to see them. There was great public fascination for these ships, for shipping, for romantic far-off lands, and for the passengers and cargos they carried. And these ships seemed to be 'serenaded' by great flotillas of support craft: barges, tugs, floating derricks. Evocatively, the ships and the well-known, quite historic shipowners themselves often represented the great might and vast expanse of the old, bygone Empire. Fascinatingly named liners, combination passenger-cargo and pure freight ships came from all corners of the earth. There might be those hardworking freighters like the *City of Madras* from Calcutta, the *Canberra Star* from Melbourne, the *Nowshera* from Zanzibar, the *Pacific Stronghold* from Vancouver. And the liners came as well – Cunard's *Saxonia* from Montreal, the *Amazon* from Rio, the *Athenic* from Wellington, the *Durban Castle* from Mombasa and the *Arcadia* from Sydney and Suva.

Unlike most other ports, however, these passenger ships in particular actually had to follow a rather unique process. Many would land their passengers and baggage at an outer dock called the Tilbury Landing Stage, located about an hour's train ride from the very heart of the capital itself. Afterwards, tugs would shift these liners to the inner London freight docks, such as the Royal Albert and King George V docks, where they would offload and then reload their lucrative cargos. And outbound, they reversed the process – another short call at Tilbury to take on fresh passengers making the out-going voyage. Alternately, some smaller passenger ships had specially routed trains to deliver their guests direct to the cargo sheds in the inner docks.

But, as in most major world ports, the shipping business changed drastically in the second half of the twentieth century. Shifts in world politics and in trading patterns have dealt severe blows, namely far fewer ships, mostly replaced by larger ones (in the container area in particular) and most of these under flags other than the Union Jack. Even many of the great shipowners are gone as well, names such as Blue Funnel, British India, Ellerman, Glen Line, New Zealand Shipping, Shaw Savill and Union Castle. And so, the Port of London grew very quiet, its pace almost silent at times, those once-teeming docks falling into sad, irretrievable decay. But some of these unused piers, indeed very useful real estate and known collectively as Docklands, have taken on new roles – one is an airport, another a high-tech office complex, still another a tourist centre. But in other places along the twists and bends of the Thames, hints of the past remain: melancholy old warehouses, silent power stations, an abandoned shipyard, unused cranes.

Cruising from London thrived for a time, however, especially in the 1980s and '90s. The former Tilbury Landing Stage, first opened in 1930 and restored in the '90s as the London International Cruise Terminal, received a steady parade of increasingly larger liners mostly in high summer. In 1993, for example, callers included the likes of the 49,000-ton *Crystal Harmony*, the 55,000-ton *Statendam* and the 34,000-ton *Crown Odyssey*. Smaller cruise ships had an alternative. They could sail farther along the river, passing the Thames Barrier, the then new Queen Elizabeth II Bridge and the old observatory and maritime museum at Greenwich. The famed Tower Bridge opened and they sailed into the centre of the city, to the so-called Pool of London. But instead of an actual terminal, ships such as the *Seabourn Pride*, the *Royal Viking Queen* and the *Song of Flower* could moor alongside a preserved Second World War warship, the HMS *Belfast*. Passengers could cross her decks and then walk ashore, minutes away from the likes of Westminster and Piccadilly. Otherwise, a plan to build an actual cruise terminal along the opposite riverbank, near the Tower of London, was then just in the planning stages. In 1992, the Port of London handled more cruise passengers than any other British port (Southampton and Dover have since surpassed London, and a record

1 million British vacationers now take cruises each year). And while London's cruise traffic declined, giving way to the more convenient likes of both Dover and Southampton and both of which can handle today's mega cruise liners, the Port of London still sees some passenger shipping. It is also the port of great romance and reflection, and a great link to many of the passenger vessels mentioned in these pages.

In a flashback, I recall a summer's evening in 1993. We were aboard the *Crystal Harmony* and had just left the Tilbury Landing Stage, but had to pause momentarily. The outbound *Enrico Costa* was already in the river, being readied by tugs for the run out into the North Sea.

Upriver, the *Royal Viking Queen* was already underway. The sight of these three liners made me pause and think back to busier days – when it might have been the *Kenya*, *City of York* and *Rhodesia Castle* that were sailing. This book is a nostalgic glance backward to the final age, in the 1950s and '60s, when British passenger ships sailed to the four corners of the earth.

Bill Miller
Secaucus, New Jersey
Summer 2008

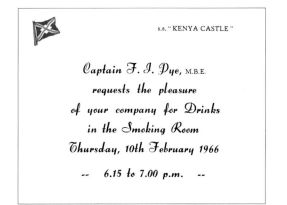

1

POST-WAR ANCHOR TRIO

The Anchor Line was rather unusual among British passenger ship lines in being based at Glasgow. Most other firms were headquartered either at London or Liverpool. Formed by clever Scot bankers, the Company's interests were primarily in the Indian trade – between Liverpool and Bombay via the Mediterranean and Suez. They maintained a transatlantic service as well, mostly to New York, but only until the outbreak of the Second World War in September 1939. These were not resumed in 1946–47, when with three sisterships, the *Circassia* (1937), *Cilicia* (1938) and *Caledonia* (1948), reopened the Indian service. One-class ships, they carried approximately 300 passengers each as well as considerable cargo. They ran a steady, popular service for some years. New tonnage was considered at times, but with a declining trade by the 1960s, Anchor decided to withdraw altogether from all passenger services. The *Circassia* made the final sailing in January 1966 and then was sold to Spanish breakers. The *Cilicia* went to Dutch buyers, who used her as the stevedores' training ship *Jan Bakx*. Moored in Rotterdam harbour, she was not scrapped until 1980. The *Caledonia* became a student hostel for the University of Amsterdam until broken-up in 1971.

The classic-looking *Caledonia* is shown here at Port Said on 20 May 1957, the first British liner to have passed through the Suez Canal since it was blocked months before, in November 1956. (Cronican-Faber Collection)

2

BIBBY TO BURMA

Although dating as far back as 1807, Bibby did not enter commercial passenger shipping for nearly another ninety years. With strong interests in the colonial run to Burma as well as in peacetime trooping (under charter to the British Government), the Company was known for its vintage-looking, four-masted combination passenger-cargo ships. By the late 1950s, the Company ran four of these combo ships – the 10,300-ton, 115 all-first-class *Worcestershire* of 1931, the similar *Derbyshire* of 1935 and then two post-war sisterships, the 8,900-ton, seventy-six-berth *Warwickshire* and *Leicestershire*. By then, there were two full-time troopers as well, the 12,700-ton *Devonshire* and, what proved to be Britain's last peacetime troopship, the 20,500-ton, 1957-built *Oxfordshire*.

Decline and then withdrawal began for Bibby's passenger services by the early 1960s. British trooping by sea ended in 1962 and so the *Devonshire* and *Oxfordshire* were sold off – the former becoming the *Devonia* for British India and thereafter used as an educational cruise ship; the latter being extensively rebuilt for the Australian and around-the-world tourist trades as Sitmar Line's *Fairstar*.

Passenger service to Rangoon ended by 1964. The *Worcestershire* had been sold to Japanese breakers in 1961 and was renamed *Kannon Maru* for her delivery voyage out to Osaka. The *Derbyshire* was scrapped at Hong Kong in 1964 while the sisters *Warwickshire* and *Leicestershire* were sold to the Greek-flag Typaldos Lines and rebuilt as the Mediterranean ferries *Hania* and *Heraklion*. Jumping to nearly 12,000 tons, they could now carry as many as 1,450 passengers, 100 autos and eighty coaches. For a short time, the *Hania* was actually listed as the largest ferry in the world. The *Heraklion* made

worldwide news, however, after sinking in the Aegean during a storm on 8 December 1966. She was lost within fifteen minutes and with 241 casualties. Eventually found to be unsafely loaded, the inquiries prompted the closure of Typaldos Lines and seizure by the Greek Government of its entire fleet. The *Hania*, laid-up from 1967 until 1971, was sold to the Kavounides Shipping Company, also Greek, and was renamed *Sirius*. She was scrapped in Greece in 1980.

The *Staffordshire*, seen here at Capetown, had only a single foremast. (Alex Duncan)

The 8,900-ton *Leicestershire* and its sister *Warwickshire* were classic British combination passenger-cargo ships with passenger and staff quarters amidships and then cargo being stowed fore and aft. (Captain James McNamara Collection)

The 498ft-long *Warwickshire* differed somewhat – she had both a foremast and aft mainmast. (World Ship Society)

Long in Greek hands, the *Sirius* (ex-*Warwickshire*) about to be broken-up at Skaramanga in Greece in 1980. (Antonio Scrimali)

Bibby Line also operated the 20,586-ton troopship *Oxfordshire*, commissioned in 1957 and chartered to the Ministry of Transport. She was sold off in 1962, however, and completely rebuilt for the Sitmar Line as the 1,910-passenger *Fairstar*. She was broken-up in India in 1997. (Richard Faber Collection)

3

BLUE FUNNEL COMBO SHIPS

In those long-ago days when ships were the only global connections, when indeed it was the 'only way to go', the length of sea voyages varied greatly. New York to England, for example, took five days on the likes of the speedy *Queen Mary* while England to South Africa on Union-Castle took two weeks. Indeed, one of the longest runs was the passage from Europe out to Australia and the Far East. These trips took four to six weeks. But it all seemed to matter far less then.

Although now gone out of the shipping business, the Liverpool-based Blue Funnel Line ran a group of sturdy-looking passenger-cargo liners, so-called combination ships, which carried up to thirty passengers each. With names derived from the glossaries of Greek mythology and with aptly distinctive blue-coloured smokestacks, they were affectionately dubbed the 'Blue Flues'. They were very popular, quite well-known ships in their time.

Grouped in two sets of four ships each, there was the *Helenus*, *Jason*, *Hector* and *Ixion*, and then the 'P Class' – the *Peleus*, *Pyrrhus*, *Patroclus* and *Perseus*. The first four sailed out of Liverpool via Port Said and then Aden to Australia – Fremantle, Adelaide, Melbourne and Sydney. The others went to Far Eastern waters: Liverpool as well as Rotterdam via Port Said to Singapore, Hong Kong, Kobe and Yokohama. Freight was expectedly their mainstay – British- and sometimes European-manufactured goods outwards and then a return with the likes of Australian meat and wool, Chinese and Japanese silks and, of course, the mass-produced goods of the Far East – the toys, other textiles and the likes of inexpensive plastic umbrellas and shoes. 'They were fine old ships, determined yet leisurely in their paces,' remembered Anne Beckwith-Wallace.

My late husband had business interests in the East, mostly at Hong Kong and often at Singapore. Consequently, every two or three years, we made what would be a three- or four-month journey. We'd catch one ship going out and then a different one coming home. I seemed to especially recall the *Perseus*. Of course, the long sea voyage was very pleasant and very restful. There was no planned entertainment, of course. Your daily life seemed to centre around meals. The dinners were particularly extended. Otherwise, the passengers would read, play card games, sometimes dance to records after dinner in the lounge and often take long afternoon naps.

The service on Blue Funnel was very smart. The stewards wore impeccably starched white jackets and which had highly polished brass buttons. Afternoon teas were done in almost grand, somewhat dramatically precise style and I recall curries being a great favourite at dinner. Of course, everyone seemed to gather beforehand for drinks and a chat in the little bar area. I also seem to remember that a canvas swimming pool was erected on the deck for the younger passengers. It was filled with seawater. There wasn't air conditioning and so port calls could be very warm. On deck, we sat under a canvas awning. At night, we often slept with open portholes and to the gentle sounds of the Mediterranean or the Indian Ocean or the China Sea.

Built in the period 1949–51, these 10,000-ton, 18-knot ships actually saw just a little more than a decade of passenger ship service. Even by the late 1950s, such ships were already in their twilight. By 1964, changing economics dictated that twelve passenger in freighter style would thereafter be the maximum on Blue Funnel Line ships. One saving grace was the elimination of a doctor needed aboard the thirty-passenger ships. International maritime regulations did not require a ship's doctor for a dozen passengers or less.

When these ships were eventually scrapped in the early '70s (ironically, often in the very same Far Eastern waters they had served), an era in ocean travel was just about over. Jets had taken the passengers and faster, more efficient containerships grabbed the freight (including those plastic umbrellas). The 'Blue Flues' became, like many others, part of maritime history.

Classic Blue Funnel design: The thirty-passenger *Ixion* is seen here, in a photo dated 6 September 1968, at Barclay Curle's repair yard at Glasgow. (Richard Faber Collection)

A close-up of the forward superstructure of the *Pyrrhus*. (Steffen Weirauch Collection)

A rather dramatic and certainly very busy photo of the 10,093-ton *Peleus* discharging cargo at Hong Kong in the early 1960s. (James L. Shaw Collection)

Another Blue Funnel ship was the 8,262-ton, 190-passenger *Centaur*, completed in 1963 for the Singapore to Fremantle service. She was the last Blue Funnel passenger ship, being sold in 1985 to become the Chinese *Hai Long*. (Richard K. Morse Collection)

4

BLUE STAR 'MEAT SHIPS' TO SOUTH AMERICA

'My family were coffee merchants and so this meant connections to Brazil. My father actually often travelled in the 1930s on the German airship *Graf Zeppelin*. It made winter trips to and from Pernambuco. But my husband and I always went by sea in later years, actually until the late 1960s.' So remembered Mrs Gemma Richardson, who was still sailing in the 1990s on modern, luxury cruise ships.

> Living in London, we had lots of choices to and from South America back then. The fastest and perhaps most luxurious way was on the *Andes*, a big ship that took two weeks to, say, Rio or Santos. At other times, we sailed on older, smaller ships. Names that come to mind include *Alcantara*, *Arlanza* and *Highland Monarch*. Once, we even took a French ship, the *Louis Lumiere*, going out and then an Argentine ship coming home. She was called the *Libertad*. But our favourites were always the Blue Star Line ships. They were quite impeccable, very cosy and so comfortable.

Owned by the enormously rich Vestey family, the so-called 'butchers of Britain', their London-headquartered Blue Star Line was well known in maritime circles for the huge blue stars painted on the ships' often oversized funnels. After the Second World War, in 1947–48 they built a splendid quartet of passenger-cargo liners – the *Argentina Star*, *Brasil Star*, *Paraguay Star* and *Uruguay Star*. Each carried about fifty passengers, all in first class and in superb comfort. They were routed from London via Lisbon, Madeira, Las Palmas and Teneriffe to Rio de Janeiro, Santos, Montevideo and finally Buenos Aires. With regularity, one of them sailed from London every two to three weeks.

Public rooms onboard included a lounge, a little bar, smoking room and, of course, a dining room. There was a sun deck for the passengers as well as a small pool. The cabins, mostly singles and doubles, almost all had private bathrooms. Some staterooms had an added pullman bunk. While the passenger trade was primarily linked to South America, and this included millionaire Argentine land barons and their families, the Blue Star ships also catered to wintertime British 'sun seekers'. They used the ships for the shorter voyages for stays at hotels and even in private homes in Portugal, the Canaries and Madeira.

These 10,700-ton ships also had seven cargo holds. Outwards from England, they carried manufactured goods – machinery and items such as British china and knitwear. But it was on the northward, homeward sailings that these ships earned their greatest revenues. These four ships, along with the rest of the large Blue Star freighter fleet, carried huge quantities of Argentine beef in their specially equipped freezer compartments. Much of this later found its way to the village butcher shop.

Almost simultaneously, both the passenger as well as the cargo trades fell away for these ships in the 1960s. The *Argentina Star* and her sisters with their fifty or so passenger berths, now often unfilled, became unprofitable. Company managers were quite content with more economical twelve-passenger freighters. And almost as a prelude to their demise, the *Paraguay Star* was swept by fire at the London Docks in August 1969. There was little interest in repairing her, of course. She was quickly sold to West German scrap merchants at Hamburg. Three years later, in 1972, the remaining three were sold to Taiwanese scrappers. Stripped and empty, they made long, lonely voyages out to their Far Eastern graves. But just before, at London, in August 1972, I recall seeing them at anchor in the Thames. Still handsome ships, they reminded me of that old passenger trade – 'Blue Star to South America'.

Blue Star Line ships were noted for their oversized funnels bearing a large blue star overlaid on a white disc. Here we see the 503ft-long *Uruguay Star* at Lisbon. (Luis Miguel Correia Collection)

The passenger lounge aboard the *Uruguay Star* had what was a very typical British style: lino flooring, burl woods, oversized chairs – some upholstered and others in leatherette. (Richard Faber Collection)

The dining room aboard the 16-knot *Brasil Star* and her three sisters had wrap-around windows that faced forward. (Richard Faber Collection)

The Belgian *Thysville*, built in 1950 for the colonial run to the Congo, was sold to the Booth Line in 1961 for a short stint on the Amazon River run as the *Anselm*. In 1963, she joined Blue Star and then sailed as their seventy-six-passenger *Iberia Star*. Again a short phase, she was sold in 1965 to the Austasia Line for Singapore-Australia service as the *Australasia*. She was broken-up in 1973. (Luis Miguel Correia Collection)

UP THE AMAZON BY BOOTH LINE

'My late husband and his family had interests in the rubber business out in the interior of Brazil. We travelled often to South America and, until the early 1960s, we often went out by sea – by the Booth Line to the Amazon,' recalled Joan Benton-Smith. A well-known British shipowner based at Liverpool and owned by the larger Blue Star Line, the Booth Steamship Co. Ltd was noted for its unique passenger and freight service to the exotic Amazon region. Apart from the British operations, a separate freighter service was run from US East Coast ports as well.

On the trade between two of the world's great rivers, the Mersey and the Amazon, Booth ran three fine passenger-cargo ships in the 1950s. The eldest, the 1931-built *Hilary*, carried 230 passengers in two classes, first and tourist, along with freight. After the Second World War, the slightly larger 7,700-ton *Hildebrand* of 1951 and then the 8,000-ton *Hubert* of 1955 were added. Modelled after Blue Star's *Argentina Star* quartet of passenger-cargo liners of the late 1940s, both the *Hildebrand* and the *Hubert* were rather unusual in their day for having their main superstructures placed farther aft than customary

The ill-fated *Hildebrand*, completed in 1951 and seen here at Southampton. She stranded along the Portugese coast in September 1957 and had to be abandoned as a complete loss. (Gillespie-Faber Collection)

Cosy and comfortable, the first-class lounge aboard the *Hubert*. (Andy Hernandez Collection)

and also for having a single, forward mast and none aft. The Booth Line houseflag was painted on their stacks and like the Company's cargo ships, such as the *Boniface*, *Clement* and *Dunstan*, were named for saints. The passenger ships were routed from Liverpool to Leixoes and Lisbon in Portugal, Funchal on Madeira, Barbados and Trinidad in what was then the British West Indies, Belem in Brazil and finally 1,000 miles along the Amazon to Manaus. The roundtrip took fifty days.

'We travelled mostly on the *Hildebrand* and then on the *Hubert* in the very final years. I remember them both as comfortable little liners,' added Mrs Benton-Smith:

The first class dining room on the *Hildebrand*, as I recall, faced on the Main Deck and had large windows on three sides facing onto the sea. It was such a pleasant setting for meals and, done up especially in blue linens, it was used for afternoon tea as well. In heavy weather, in the Bay of Biscay in particular and sometimes in the mid-Atlantic, the dining room windows were fitted with steel covers. Above was the main lounge and the smoking room, which were smartly decorated, but still had a cosy, almost club-like feel at the same time. Clearly, the decoration was unlike the big liners, which sometimes tended to overpower their passenger-guests.

The first class staterooms [seventy-four berths in all on the *Hubert*] were also well appointed. I especially remember that the doors were fitted with screens for maximum ventilation in that very hot weather that was so common to the Amazon region. In every room, there was a detailed map of the Amazon River and a copy of these were given to each passenger at the end of a voyage. The ladies were also given a special gift – a silver compact with the Booth Line crest on it.

Tourist class [ninety-six berths] was aft and had more restrained decor. There was only cold running water in the cabins, for example.

Unfortunately, the *Hildebrand* – which had represented her owners at the great Coronation Fleet Review for Queen Elizabeth II in June 1953 – was wrecked off the Portuguese coast in September 1957. The veteran *Hilary* went to the scrapheap in 1960. The 437ft-long *Hubert* sailed alone until, by October 1964, economics ended the passenger service between Liverpool and the Amazon. The 15-knot ship was transferred within the parent Blue Star Group to a Singapore-based subsidiary, the Austasia Line. Renamed *Malaysia*, she sailed for some ten years in passenger-cargo service between western Australian ports and Singapore. In 1976, she was rebuilt as the livestock carrier *Khaleej Express*, hoisted the Saudi Arabian colours and worked the Australia-Middle East sheep trade. She went to Pakistani shipbreakers in 1984.

By the 1970s, Booth services were run by small freighters, most of which flew 'flags of convenience'. Today, the Booth name is but a memory. They no longer trade as a British shipping line. But the Amazon region has come into its own with passengers. Now, large, often very large, all-white cruise ships make the two and a half-day journey to and from Manaus and the open Atlantic with almost weekly regularity in deep winter (the South American summer, of course). 'It was a great adventure back in the 1950s,' concluded Mrs Benton-Smith. 'In ways, it was the most unique voyage then offered on a British passenger ship. I remember the Booth ships with great affection!'

A near-sister, the 8,062-ton *Hubert* of 1955 finished her days in a rather unusual role: carrying sheep as the Middle Eastern-owned *Khaleej Express*. (Albert Wilhelmi Collection)

Equally intimate and rather charming, the first-class smoking room aboard the *Hildebrand*. (Andy Hernandez Collection)

BRITISH INDIA AND THE LAST OF THE EMPIRE

When, at the age of sixteen, in 1960, young Terry Russell joined the cadet cargo ship *Chindwara* of the illustrious British India Steam Navigation Co. Ltd, BI for short, he found his baggage strapped to the ship's funnel. Such were the initiations of an apprentice, about to steam off to the realities of a career at sea. When we met, some twenty-five years later, Terry Russell was Deputy Captain Russell, second in command of the P&O liner *Oriana*, then the world's fifth largest liner and cruising full-time from Sydney, Australia.

The name itself, British India, stirs up images of the imperial past, of a distant time, an evocative and in some ways romantic bygone era. British India and its fleet were for decades a very important connection to the British Empire and its last remnants. Their ships were vital links not just for the exchange of important cargos (British-manufactured goods going outwards, the local items and prized minerals coming home), but also for the steady, seemingly uninterrupted flow of the representatives of the Crown: the governors and high commissioners, the police and troops, their families, the traders, clergy and, of course, even the occasional tourist.

Russell's grandfather, father and brother had all gone to sea. He himself joined British India because, aside from the New Zealand Shipping Co., it was the only British shipping firm with cadet training ships. The 7,500-ton *Chindwara* carried a regular crew of fifty-three, but then also forty-six cadets, who were, in fact, the ship's deck crew. It was a four-year training course. 'The *Chindwara* sailed from London's Royal Albert Dock on three and a half-month roundtrips to either India or South and East Africa,' he recalled. 'Outbound, we'd take general cargo: cars, refrigerators and machinery. Homeward, we would have tea, cobra, spices, bone meal and sissel.'

Until the late 1960s, London-based British India retained an enormous network of passenger as well as freight services. 'The Company had its own "foreign service", which meant two and a half years in India.

Every officer was given a Hindustani book and expected to acquire at least a working knowledge of Hindi,' said Captain Russell.

Actually, many of the officers became quite proficient. One often transferred between ships, which were based at either Bombay or Calcutta, and which therefore meant a long, often uncomfortable train ride across India. Home leave to Britain included passage in an available Company freighter. There were no crew flights in those days. Also, there were special British India Clubs in Bombay and Calcutta, and even British India flats in places like Hong Kong and Singapore. Officers could bring out their families for their stints of 'foreign service'. Indeed, British India was, in many ways, a great remnant, the last of the old empire.

British India's passenger ship fleet was quite diverse in those years. According to Captain Russell:

All of our passenger ships carried at least two or three classes as well as considerable freight. The sisters *Kenya* and *Uganda* worked the East African trade out of London and sailed via Suez. Other ships sailed from Bombay to the Seychelles, East Africa and up to the Persian Gulf, and still others from Calcutta to Southeast Asia and the Far East. The most prized run was, however, on the little 2,200-ton *Mombasa*, which was based at Mombasa and sailed on a regular schedule to Tanga, Zanzibar, Dar-es-Salaam, Lindi and Mtwara. *Mombasa* was a favourite port for assignment and we even kept a special BI tug there. 'Mtwara and the Nut Trade' was well known within the British India fleet.

British India, while linked to P&O from 1914, was not fully integrated into the giant P&O Group until 1971. According to Captain Russell:

This coincided with British India's rapid decline and subsequent demise. There was an enormous shift in trade and a general move to more and more charters.

Pride of the post-war British India fleet, the *Kenya* originally had a black hull and differed from her sister *Uganda* in having a shorter funnel. (British India Line)

The taller funnel aboard the somewhat mightier-looking *Uganda* is evident in this view at the Royal Docks, London, in 1956. (Young & Sawyer Collection)

Container shipping was also then spreading worldwide. There was also a rapid rise in national shipping, namely some African-flag firms and, of course, the big Shipping Corporation of India. Our passenger trade disappeared as well. Initially, the traditional first class business vanished, but then the once lucrative third class traffic turned to air flights as well. Furthermore, there were swift political and social changes, particularly in 'new' self-governing East Africa. The colonial days were indeed over and the last links of the old Empire being severed. All of this was compounded as our fleet grew older, more expensive and was even complicated by the sudden closure of the Suez Canal in 1967.

Interestingly, however, even in its final years, British India ships proved to be a marvellous training ground for today's maritime management of East Africa, Malaysia, Kuwait, the Gulf Arab States, Ceylon and India. Many of their port ministers and shipping superintendents began as cadets on BI.

Captain Russell also served in British India's specialised, well-reputed educational cruising program:

I began on the old *Devonia* and *Dunera* in 1965. They were 12,700-tonners that carried some 190 adults in cabin accommodations and over 800 youngsters in huge dormitories. On these ships, our entertainment equipment consisted of one record player per ship. We created all other events. At best, these ships, which dated from the late '30s, did 12 knots. In fact, the *Devonia* was fitted with the Sulzer diesels that had been exhibited at the 1931 Geneva Industrial Fair. The ships were cooled by the old Punkah forced air system. The adult passengers had

the services of a wonderful Indian bath steward. My own cabin opened onto the deck and so I had to go along just to get a bath.

Later, I served in the 20,500-ton *Nevasa*, a British India troopship, which became a very popular schools cruiseship. However, the last of this cruising group, the 16,700-ton *Uganda*, was the most beloved of all. She had great charm and established a very strong rapport with passengers of all ages. When P&O closed out the British India educational cruise program in 1983, it was a deep loss to many travellers. I was most fortunate to have served in these ships.

Captain Russell also served in the well-known D Class of passenger ships on the Persian Gulf run from Bombay to Karachi and such ports as Muscat, Dubai, Umm Said, Bahrain, Bushire, Kuwait and Basrah.

There were four, 4,800-ton sisterships – the *Dara*, *Daressa*, *Dumra* and *Dwarka* – all built in the late 1940s. They carried about sixty cabin passengers and over 1,000 in deck class. Our diversity in passengers was therefore quite extreme, from Middle Eastern royalty in cabin class – and complete with their own entourages of servants, cooks and bodyguards – to migrant workers and religious pilgrims in the unberthed section. The *Dara* was lost by terrorist explosion and then fire, however, in April 1961. It was a tragedy that claimed 200 lives. The other ships were later sold off and then scrapped, victims of a declining trade. When the *Dwarka*, the last of the quartet, was retired in the spring of 1982, she was the last of the British India passenger ships to be based overseas. It was the end of a long, rich history. The curtain had come down!

The 14,430-ton *Uganda* was rebuilt in 1967–68 as an educational cruise ship. (Michael Cassar Collection)

The *Karanja* and her sister *Kampala*, dating from 1947–48, were among the most popular and best known of the vast, post-war British India passenger fleet. (Alex Duncan)

Terry Russell later joined the P&O passenger fleet, serving aboard such liners as the *Himalaya*, *Arcadia*, *Oriana* and then on affiliate Princess cruise ships *Sun Princess* and *Pacific Princess*.

BI SISTERS

The sisters *Kenya* and *Uganda* were perhaps British India's best-known post-war passenger ships. In 1985, the *Uganda* finished her career – in the silent abandonment of some Far Eastern scrapyard – and so concluded the story of these fine ships. The *Kenya* had been in service until June 1969, running the last British-flag passenger service out of what had been colonial East Africa. By then, however, with decolonization well underway, both the passenger and freight trades had withered substantially. That once bright sun for British passenger shipping, once the largest network on earth, was indeed setting.

The 14,400-ton *Kenya* and *Uganda* had, in fact, been built for a very specific trade. According to Hans Andresen, a frequent passenger and resident of East Africa:

In the late 1940s, Britain had put millions into the ground nut scheme in Tanganyika. The port of Mtwara was especially created for an expected large flow of both passengers and freight. Therefore, the *Kenya* and *Uganda* were built, as especially large passenger-cargo ships, for this trade [from London to Gibraltar, Port Said, the Suez Canal, Aden, Mombasa, Tanga, Zanzibar, Dar-es-Salaam, Beira and then turnaround at Durban].

Built to carry about 175 passengers in first class and 125 in tourist class, they catered mostly to European travellers, a few Asians and even fewer Africans. They had beautifully finished interiors with very fine woods. Various African artefacts had also been fitted on the ships, such as the tusks on the *Uganda* and the tribal drums on the *Kenya*. There were two first class public rooms that I especially recall. It was all leather fittings in the Smoking Room and soft upholstery in the Lounge. The restaurant was thoughtfully air-conditioned and therefore a very popular space. My wife and I liked these two ships very much. They were quiet and elegant, and originally had a European dance band, but which was later replaced by an Indian band. The bandleader on the *Uganda* was Sonny Soweto, who had been recruited from Bombay and was something of a 'legend' within the British India fleet.

C.M. Squarey, the late British passenger ship connoisseur, was most enthusiastic in his descriptions of then brand new *Kenya*, written in September 1951.

The *Kenya*, unless I am mistaken, is positively 'pavements ahead,' and others will agree when I claim it is not exaggeration to say 'streets ahead,' of anything previously built by the British India Line. She is indeed so very, very good that, whilst it might be more excessive to say she can be ranked as a challenge to air transport, nevertheless, I dare predict that her delightful qualities and quarters will succeed in enticing more than a few people living in East Africa who have become rather air-minded for their home leave, to think twice before taking to the air next time and, instead, say to themselves, 'Let's go by the *Kenya* next home leave and really relax, rest and recuperate'.

The 8,908-ton, 479ft-long *Santhia* anchored in Hong Kong harbour. (British India Line)

Mr Squarey also wrote, as part of the conclusion of his appraisal:

The finish and general workmanship on this ship impressed me very much and, furthermore, her delivery date was kept – and she was delivered a completely finished ship [from Barclay, Curle Shipyards of Glasgow]. Despite being very light in the water, she ran smoothly [during an inaugural, invited-guests-only cruise from Glasgow to London], and even at the stern end vibration was virtually nil. Designed for a service speed of 16 knots, she touched over 19 knots on trials.

Brian Gregory, the chief engineer aboard the *Queen Elizabeth II*, served in his earlier sea-going years onboard the *Uganda*. 'Ships like the *Uganda* offered a gentile lifestyle,' he remembered.

There weren't any entertainers onboard, for example, in those days. The officers and the passengers joined together to create diversions and amusements. Some 50% of our passengers were British Government civil servants and their families, and then only a few tourists. In later years, as commercial air routes developed, the fathers of these families would fly, but the mothers and the children would continue to go by sea. Of course, in the very end, they too had deserted to aircraft.

Cargo was, quite expectedly, very important to the economics of a ship like the *Uganda* and her sister, the *Kenya*. We tended to carry general freight outbound and then return from East Africa with frozen meat, spices, sissel and butter from Kenya. In those days, long before the current age of quick-turnaround containerships, we spent fourteen days in London's Royal Albert Docks – five or six days for discharge and then seven to load.

While there had been some thought in the late 1960s to rebuilding the *Kenya* as either a cruise ship or floating industrial display ship, she was sold in the end to Italian shipbreakers at La Spezia. She was dismantled in the summer of 1969. Earlier, in 1967–68, the *Uganda*, which had been withdrawn from the East African trade, was converted at Hamburg to a specialty schools' cruise ship, carrying 306 adults and 920 students housed in separate quarters. She cruised, mostly on two-week trips to the Mediterranean, and to enormous popularity. She was used, however, as a hospital ship during the Falklands War in 1982, but, as she was an aging ship with then declining passenger loads, she spent her final years – after a very brief return to commercial cruising – as a military replenishment ship in the South Atlantic.

The *Uganda*, the last colonial liner in the British fleet, was laid-up in Cornwall's River Fal in the spring of 1985. At least one preservationist group hoped to keep her as a museum ship, but, once again, economics played a decisive part in the scheme of things. A year later, she was sold to a Jamaica-based intermediary, renamed *Triton* and then set off from Falmouth, on 20 May, for the slow, final voyage

to Taiwanese scrappers at Kaohsiung. Keith Byass, the noted British maritime photographer, witnessed the final departure of this last British India liner. 'It was a very moving experience, bags of tears, car horns blowing, etc.,' he wrote. 'The rust on her hull was a sorry sight and, as she got underway, her black smoke nearly blotted out the entire scene.' Once at Taiwan, however, the former *Uganda* – while awaiting a berth at the scrapper's yard – was driven aground by Typhoon Wayne and then heeled over on her side. What a sad ending!

Glorious ships, the British India *Kenya* and *Uganda* were reflections of a lost era – of midnight sailings from Mombasa and cargo holds filled with spice and sissel, and of colonial high commissioners sitting in lounges with wickerwork chairs and overhead fans while sipping midday gins.

SCHOOLSHIP CRUISING

'I especially remember the greasy and queasy breakfasts. Everything was fried in grease that was a half-inch deep,' recalled Alex and Mhairi Lang of Port Glasgow. As youngsters, they'd sailed in 1963 on two British India schools cruises – Alex aboard the *Dunera*, Mahairi on her near-sister, the *Devonia*. Originally troopships built in the late '30s, they ran these educational cruises exclusively in their later years. Sensible-looking motorships with single stacks and all-white hulls, they offered a variety of itineraries. Alex Lang's thirteen-day trip departed from Grangemouth for Hamburg, Stockholm, Visby, Copenhagen, Oslo and Kristiansand; Mhairi's was a shorter run, from Greenock via Belfast to Corunna, Lisbon and Vigo.

'My trip cost £36 for two weeks,' recalled Alex.

There were twelve boys to a dormitory and we were in the bow section. There were sixteen each in the girls' dormitories. The bunks were two high. There were also little 'fights' between the dormitories. We'd push things under the partitions, especially since there was an ongoing competition for points for the cleanest, neatest dorms. There was reveille in the morning. They played a sea shanty. During my two-week cruise, we had four days at sea. We would have classes, one in the morning and one in the afternoon. We'd learn bits of a foreign language and have lectures on history and geography. We had bus tours in every port and we were given 2s each per port for spending money. We would also have free time in the ports, but with a very specified return time. At the onset, they always showed us exactly where the ship was docked. Our girls danced on the quayside at Lisbon accompanied by bagpipes.

I seem to recall that we had Granny Smith apples at every lunch or dinner. After dinner, it was 'lights out' at about 10 o'clock. Some of the students were, of course, seasick. I remember one was seasick for the entire trip.

Completed in 1926, the 8,496-ton *Rajula* had a very long career. Sold to the Shipping Corporation of India in 1973 and renamed *Rangat*, she survived for another two years before going to Bombay breakers. This meant a career of forty-nine years. (British India Line)

The 5,030-ton *Dara*, built just after the Second World War in 1948, was one of the four 'D Class' sisters built for the Bombay-Karachi-Persian Gulf run. (British India Line)

The small, 2,213-ton *Mombasa* worked the East African coastal run between Mombasa and Mtwara. She carried eight in first class, sixteen in second class and 250 on deck. (British India Line)

British India schools' cruising was immensely popular for many years and included voyages on the 1937-built former troopship *Dunera* and her near-sister, the *Devonia*, the former *Devonshire* of the Bibby Line. (Luis Miguel Correia Collection)

A very popular ship, the 20,527-ton *Nevasa*, built as a peacetime troopship in 1956, was rebuilt for schools' cruising in 1964-65. A subsequent victim of rising fuel oil prices, she was prematurely broken-up in 1975. (Luis Miguel Correia Collection)

The late Dean Miller was P&O's public relations representative at Vancouver for some forty years. In 1980, he travelled aboard the *Uganda*. 'She had great charm, pure charm in the passenger section,' he recalled following a two-week Eastern Mediterranean cruise from Venice.

> There was overall elegance. The dining room seemed to be at least two decks high with its cove ceiling. It was very handsome, very classical. The salon, the main lounge, had mounted elephant tusks. On an aft deck was a large auditorium. Thirty or forty seats on top were reserved for the adult passengers to enjoy the very fine lecturers, who spoke mostly on history. The *Uganda* carried the old time British passengers including lots of great characters and a few eccentrics. Many of them had been in high positions and there was Dame this and Lady that. The *Uganda* was also a training ground for younger officers bound for the larger P&O liners.

Ship's photographer Ian Noble served aboard the 540ft-long *Uganda* in 1984, her final schoolship days. She had just finished a long stint of service for the British Government – first as a hospital ship in the Falklands War of 1982 and then as a South Atlantic transport and supply ship. 'She was still a ship of two distinct worlds – upper decks for the adult passengers and the remainder of the ship for the students. The lower decks even smelt like a school,' he recalled. 'There was a

headmaster and headmistress. Typically, the headmaster wore a long gown. The 900 kids were very segregated from the adults except for the excellent lectures. Some of the little ports, such as ones in the Mediterranean, seemed overwhelmed by all those youngsters.'

'The *Uganda*'s adult passengers were of an old era, in fact the last of an old era,' recalled Noble. 'I remember that they used to tip the Indian lift operator. He opened and closed a gate all day. My Goanese cabin steward had worked for the P&O [and affiliates like British India] for fifty years. He polished shoes, cooked breakfast, ran errands. He too was from an old era.'

'The adults' lounge had wood panelling and leather seats. It was all like a club, a home away from home,' he added. 'The kids came from all different schools – some in uniforms like grey skirts and blue blazers and others from the inner cities and who were often caught sneaking cigarettes. As the photographer, I would take group pictures of thirty to forty kids at a time.'

Ian Noble did the very last cruise, which ended at Malta in the spring of 1985. 'The very last night was very sad, very emotional,' he said. 'There was a huge disco party. The Captain [John Branford] was even in tears. The *Uganda* then went empty back to the UK and was laid-up at Falmouth. Several years later, I saw it on its side at Kaohsiung. She was broken in two. Later [1996], I heard that she was in four or five pieces.'

7

CANADIAN PACIFIC DAYS

In 2006, a glossy new hardcover appeared in the bookshops of Canada. It consisted of a collection of evocative posters of the Canadian Pacific Co. It was a firm that once ranked as the most extensive transportation system in the world. There were trains, planes, hotels and mountain resorts, lake steamers and – most intriguing to my eye – the great liners. Mostly, these consisted of the romantic Empress ships. But then there were also the Duchess liners of the 1920s and the West Coast Princess 'boats'. Those long bygone ships hint of another age, even that long-demolished British Empire (Canadian Pacific Steamships was, after all, a Liverpool-based firm) with names such as *Empress of Britain*, *Empress of Australia*, *Empress of Canada* and *Empress of England*. Other ships' names hinted of the Company's great geographic range – *Empress of France*, *Empress of Japan*, even *Empress of Russia*.

The final great and grand period for the big Empress liners was in the 1950s. Afterwards, they were rather hard hit by airline competition and by the high costs of running British-flag ocean liners. From the end of the Second World War, the Company had run a two-class service across the North Atlantic between Liverpool, Greenock, Quebec City and finally Montreal (St John, New Brunswick, was substituted in the winter when the otherwise scenic St Lawrence was ice-choked). The 1950s fleet was highlighted by two pre-war liners, the *Empress of Scotland*, completed in 1930 and which was then one of the last three-stackers, and the smaller *Empress of Canada* and *Empress of France*. After the *Empress of Canada* burned out and capsized at her Liverpool berth in January 1953, a temporary relief ship, the *Empress of Australia*, built in 1924 as the French *De Grasse*, was used. Then there were three brand new liners: the *Empress of Britain* in 1956, the *Empress of England* a year later and finally the *Empress of Canada*. She was Company's last liner and was completed in 1961.

Bernard Chabot, president of Miami-based Admiral Cruises in the 1980s, sailed Canadian Pacific on those still busy transatlantic crossings in the '50s:

I served on the *Empress of Scotland*, which was the pre-war *Empress of Japan* and the fastest liner on the Pacific in the 1930s. I worked in the onboard railway office, selling tickets to passengers. We booked them on trains all over North America and on the 'boat trains' between Liverpool and London. Onboard at night in those days, we had to wear a tux and dance. But first, we had to pass the purser's office inspections – fingernails and hair and pressed trousers.

'The onboard feel and tone were more of transport. Nowadays, it is all pleasure,' he added. 'We had a storage room, for example, where passengers could make daily visits to their steamer trunks. The trip was usually four and a half days out of Liverpool and then a day or so in the St Lawrence.'

In winters, when the North Atlantic was cold and dreary and quite empty of most passengers, the *Empress of Scotland* went cruising from New York. 'Mostly, we did thirteen-day Caribbean trips then, with an overnight in New York each trip,' remembered Chabot.

Life onboard even for all-first class cruises had its routine. There was 4 o'clock high teas followed by cocktails with quiet music. It was all very subdued and tranquil. There was only mild entertainment after dinner. It was all early-to-bed and early-to-rise. There was lots of promenade deck strolling, deck games and reading in deckchairs. Onboard the *Empress of Scotland*, we had forced-air ventilation and a canvas, portable pool, but it was rarely used. It was more to splash or a quick cooling-off. It was all very civilized. The food was, of course, very good and there was lots of it. There were also these gala buffets, a kind of gastronomic decadence. Almost every night was formal. It was classier then – long gowns and dancing and soft music. Certainly, they were more romantic times – those long-ago Canadian Pacific days.

By 1957, the *Queen Mary*, the *Queen of Bermuda* and the *Empress of Scotland* were the last three-stackers in the British passenger fleet. The former *Empress of Japan* of 1930, she would soon be rebuilt and modernised, however, as the twin-funnel West German *Hanseatic*. (Roger Sherlock)

The splendid first-class main lounge aboard the *Empress of Scotland* in the 1950s. (Richard Faber Collection)

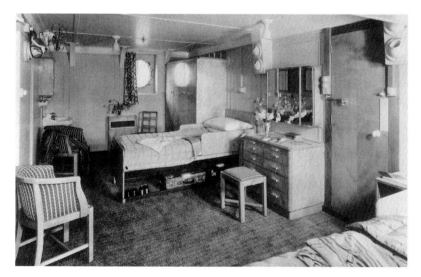

A very spacious first-class, double-bedded cabin. (Richard Faber Collection)

The ill-fated *Empress of Canada*, built in 1928 as the *Duchess of Richmond* and then restored after the Second World War, burned out at her Liverpool berth on 25 January 1953. Sadly, she was beyond economic repair. (Cronican-Arroyo Collection)

The *Empress of France*, the former *Duchess of Bedford* and with modernised funnels, seen here in the Mersey at Liverpool in 1959. She was broken-up a year later. (F. Leonard Jackson Collection)

Righting the capsized *Empress of Canada* was a long and complicated affair. We see her remains in the Gladstone Dock at Liverpool. (J.K. Byass)

To quickly replace the burnt-out *Empress of Canada* to especially heavy Coronation Year traffic in 1953, Canadian Pacific quickly purchased the French Line's 17,700-ton *De Grasse*, which was renamed *Empress of Australia*. She was sold by 1956, however, becoming the Italian *Venezuela* and then was badly damaged by grounding in 1960 and finally scrapped in 1962. (Richard Faber Collection)

Having been named by Her Majesty Queen Elizabeth II, the *Empress of Britain* – Canadian Pacific's new post-war flagship – goes down the ways at the Fairfield Shipbuilding yard at Glasgow on 22 June 1955. (Cronican-Arroyo Collection)

Seen departing from Montreal, the 640ft-long *Empress of England* and her sister were, for a time, very popular on the two-class North Atlantic run. (Cronican-Arroyo Collection)

The last Empress liners were hard-hit by both airline competition and the rising costs of operating British-flag passenger ships in the 1960s. The veteran, 1928-built *Empress of France*, was sold to scrappers in December 1960 and broken-up at Newport in Monmouthshire. The far newer, 1956-built *Empress of Britain* was sold to the Greek Line in 1964 and refitted as their *Queen Anna Maria*. She went to Carnival Cruise Lines in 1975 and became the *Carnivale* and later the *Fiesta Marina* before going to the Epirotiki Lines of Greece, who sailed her as the *Olympic*. She sailed until April 2008 as the Greek-owned *The Topaz*, but mostly under charter for Japanese educational cruises around the world. She was broken-up in India in the summer of 2008. Her sister, the *Empress of England*, was sold to the Shaw Savill Line in 1970, becoming their *Ocean Monarch* before being scrapped in 1975. Finally, the last of the Canadian Pacific liners, the *Empress of Canada*, ended the Company's transatlantic sailings in November 1971. She then became the *Mardi Gras* for Carnival Cruise Lines until 1993, when she was renamed *Star of Texas* and then *Lucky Star* before joining Epirotiki Lines as the *Apollon*. She ended her days at the hands of Indian scrappers in spring 2003.

The first-class sun lounge onboard the *Empress of Britain*. (Albert Wilhelmi Collection)

Poetic view: the *Empress of Britain* and Cunard's *Britannic* at the Landing Stage at Liverpool in 1959. (Albert Wilhelmi Collection)

Again onboard the 1,054-passenger *Empress of Britain* – the vast sports deck. (Albert Wilhelmi Collection)

Festive looking in her Carnival Cruise Lines' colours, the former *Empress of Britain* became the *Carnivale* for Miami-Caribbean sailings in 1975. Previously, between 1964 and 1975, she had been the Greek Line's *Queen Anna Maria*. (Luis Miguel Correia Collection)

Having reached her fiftieth year in 2006, the *Empress of Britain* went on to become Carnival's *Fiesta*, then Epirotiki's *Olympic*, and then as *The Topaz* before being scrapped in 2008. (Michael Cassar)

Seen here leaving Liverpool, the 650ft-long *Empress of Canada*, completed in 1961, was the last of the great Canadian Pacific liners. (F. Leonard Jackson Collection)

First in the Carnival Cruise Lines' fleet, the *Mardi Gras* (ex-*Empress of Canada*) is seen here at Nassau. (Luis Miguel Correia Collection)

8

CUNARD: WHEN GETTING THERE WAS HALF THE FUN

Following the ravages and turmoil of the Second World War, the giant Cunard Steamship Co. Ltd had little interest in building further super liners. Their two biggest and fastest ships, the *Queen Mary* (completed in 1936) and the *Queen Elizabeth* (delivered in grey war paint four years later), were quite able to handle the express runs between New York, Cherbourg and Southampton. Otherwise, Cunard would be, or so it seemed, content with more moderately sized tonnage. Their New York runs also employed the 35,000-ton *Mauretania*, the 27,000-ton *Britannic*, the 13,000-ton combination sisterships *Media* and *Parthia* and, on occasion, the big, 34,000-ton cruise ship *Caronia*. The Company's separate Canadian service, to the St Lawrence River ports of Quebec City and later Montreal, was looked after by four, rather elderly passenger ships – the *Ascania*, *Franconia*, *Samaria* and *Scythia*. All of them were, however, growing tired and increasingly troublesome. Therefore, plans were made for some new, much improved tonnage on this route. The first announcement came just before Christmas of 1951: 'Two of the largest Cunarders ever built specifically for the steamship line's Canadian service are to be constructed by the John Brown shipyards of Clydeside'. More realistically, the two ships – and in an order that was later extended to two more sisters – were placed in size at 22,000 tons, which in fact was quite an average size compared to earlier Cunarders and those of the rival Canadian Pacific fleet. They would appear at almost yearly intervals, between 1954 and 1957, as the *Saxonia*, *Ivernia*, *Carinthia* and *Sylvania*.

After carrying some two million troops during the war, the *Queens* were restored in 1946–47. 'I used to go out in launches to meet the great liners at Southampton. Cunard was the elite of British shippers back then. They were the head of the kingdom in ways. It was considered very secure just to work for them, sort of like the Bank of England up in London,' recalled the late John Crabb, a Southampton-based shipping company agent for some fifty years.

I saw both *Queens* refurbished after heavy and heroic war service. They were the showcases of Britain in the late '40s, but of course all the provisions came from the USA. Britain itself was caught up in very strict rationing. There would be three boat trains down from London for every trip of the *Queens*. We had all the celebrities: the Queen Mother, Winston Churchill, Rita Hayworth, David Niven. I remember the *Queen Elizabeth* getting stuck for a while in the mud. At first, we fought a losing battle to free her. It was all rather embarrassing to Cunard. The old *Aquitania* was still about, but she was a different era even from the two *Queens*. She was in austerity service, carrying mostly immigrants and GI wives. And we had the *Georgic*, which had been badly damaged by bombing and fires in the War, but was repaired and also in austerity service. Her bulkheads were all bent. Then we had the brand new *Caronia*. She was well liked and not only by passengers, but by the crew as well. She carried lots of old, rich ladies, who always seemed to stay at the Polygon [a now long-demolished Southampton hotel].

In the final heyday of the latter 1950s, Cunard had no less than twelve liners on the North Atlantic – the *Queen Mary* and *Queen Elizabeth*, *Mauretania*, *Caronia* on occasion, *Britannic*, *Media* and *Parthia*, the sisters *Saxonia*, *Ivernia*, *Carinthia* and *Sylvania*, and the *Scythia*. Fares for the five-day crossings on the *Queens*, as an example, were posted at $375 in first class, $225 in cabin class and $150 in tourist. Cunard was said to carry a third of all transatlantic passengers and their ships often booked a year in advance.

John Butt served on many of the Cunarders of the 1950s. 'The *Queen Mary* was absolutely the most prestigious ship in the fleet,' he said.

Even the *Queen Elizabeth* did not have the same 'magic' as the *Mary*. The *Mary* had the most superb woods in first class. She was equal to the best hotels in London and New York. But the class divisions were quite dramatic back then.

Down in tourist class, it was not quite as comfortable. It was more transport. They had 78rpm records for dancing rather than the live band up in first class.

The jet set of the day went on the *Queens*. In the Cunard offices on Lower Regent Street, there were featured photos of celebrities on the *Queen Mary* and *Queen Elizabeth*. There was Bob Hope, Charlie Chaplin, Judy Garland and Laurence Harvey. Myself, I recall ex-President Eisenhower, who was going to Britain as a private guest of the Queen, queuing up for bingo cards, and Elizabeth Taylor being impeccable to the staff. We also carried the Queen Mother [in October 1954] to and from New York. She had huge charm and an enormous sense of kindness. She'd always have a drink, a large gin and Dubonnet, before lunch. But I also remember the Soviet diplomats, who sat in the rooms all day and never left, and who were always difficult at immigration.

John Butt served on many other Cunarders of the day as well.

The *Britannic* would do long Mediterranean cruises in the winter and which were very popular in the 1950s. She carried older, wealthier passengers on those trips. Otherwise, on the Liverpool-New York run, she carried lots of freight, using all eight hatches. She was, of course, the last of the White Star ships and always flew both flags – Cunard and then White Star at times, then White Star on top and then Cunard at others. The little, 250-passenger *Media* and *Parthia*, also on the Liverpool-New York run, were originally designed as freighters. After the War, the steel was allocated to Cunard for these two ships – one for Cunard and one for the Brocklebank Line [a Cunard subsidiary]. But they were redesigned and two decks were added for passengers. They had a very loyal following which included a famous English racehorse owner who named his best horse *Parthia*. The old *Samaria* and *Ascania* were called the 'Sam' and 'Ashcan' and were used on the Canadian run. They both had great character, especially in their first class restaurants. The *Ascania* was sent from Southampton with troops in 1956 and diverted to Cyprus for the Suez Crisis. She came home and then went to scrap.

John Butt also served on the *Saxonia* and her three sisters, the *Ivernia*, *Carinthia* and *Sylvania*, built in 1954–57 and which proved to be the last Cunarders created purposely for year-round North Atlantic service.

These ships were especially designed, with a lower mast and domed funnel, to clear the bridge on the St Lawrence and turnaround at Montreal. They were built mostly for immigrants going westbound and American tourists and college students going east. It was also hoped that they would carry New Englanders. They were smaller ships, but had a certain atmosphere. But they were quickly overtaken by the airlines and also, as Britain stabilized in the 1960s, immigration to Canada dropped.

The largest liner in the world in her day, the 83,673-ton *Queen Elizabeth* is seen here in this dramatic view at Southampton dated 1949. At the upper right is the British troopship *Empire Orwell*, the former German liner *Pretoria*. (Albert Wilhelmi Collection)

The jet proved unbeatable, however, even to the likes of Cunard and so, by the early 1960s, the Company and its ships began an increasingly struggle. 'We were looking for something new, more profitable alternatives. We thought of using the *Mauretania* in year-round Caribbean service in 1962, but she was too big,' added Butt.

There would be too many launch ports. So instead, we placed her in Mediterranean-New York service and hoped to carry lots of Italian immigrants. But we were not allowed to carry Italian immigrants, which all went on either the Italian Line or American Export Lines. So, the *Mauretania* lost money and then was sold for scrap. She completed her last trip at Southampton, in November 1965, and then was stripped of her furniture. Some artefacts actually went to other ships. She was the cleanest ship ever to go to a scrapyard. About 200 crew were on the last trip, a two-day voyage up to Inverkeithing.

There were massive redundancies in 1966–67, following the big maritime strike. There was a wholesale reduction in the fleet by the end of 1968. The *Queen Mary* and *Queen Elizabeth* were gone along with the *Caronia*, *Carinthia* and *Sylvania*. Suddenly, we had one-third the office size. The Company had moved from Liverpool to Southampton and then was bought out by Trafalgar House. We felt dispirited. We'd lost the last. We'd been taken over. And we became more a name than a firm. It wasn't quite Cunard any longer.

Above An evocative evening view of the glorious *Queen Elizabeth* at the Ocean Terminal, Southampton. (J.K. Byass Collection)

Left Overnight at the Ocean Terminal, the *Queen Mary* rests between her transatlantic relays between Southampton, Cherbourg and New York. (Richard Faber Collection)

GREEN GODDESS: THE *CARONIA*

When Cunard commissioned the 34,000-ton *Caronia* in late 1948, she made headlines around the world. There seemed to be any number of distinctions about her to attract, interest, even intrigue the press. As a very large ship at that time, the 715ft-long liner was a symbol of pride and recovery, being not only the biggest, but the most luxurious passenger ship to be built in Britain since the end of the Second World War. In the age of classic two- and even three-stackers, she was the height of modernity: the largest single-stacker then afloat. She also had the tallest mast yet to go to sea. She was painted entirely in shades of green, four in all, and was immediately nicknamed the 'Green Goddess'. But most importantly, in a vision of the far-off future of the passenger ship industry, she was the first major liner to be built especially for cruising rather than crossing.

A magnificent ship in every way, she had been built by the renowned John Brown shipyards in Scotland, creators of such legendary ships as the *Lusitania*, *Aquitania* and, of course, the greatest pair of express liners ever to sail, the *Queen Mary* and *Queen Elizabeth*. While John Brown also built Canadian Pacific's dual-purpose *Empress of Britain* in 1931, they also built the *Queen Elizabeth II*, completed in 1969. The 22-knot *Caronia* appropriately had a royal baptism – she was named by Princess Elizabeth, heiress to the British throne. Soon after, in January 1949, the flag-bedecked liner arrived at New York's Pier 90, then Cunard's very own terminal. Immediately, she established a sailing pattern that would followed year after year. This helped establish her sense of clubby familiarity. In January, she cruised around the world or around the Pacific for ninety or so days. In spring, she went to the Mediterranean for about six weeks and then, in summer, to Scandinavia for some forty-five days. In autumn, she was back in the Mediterranean, this time for eight weeks. All her cruises departed from New York, but then, rather unique to Cunard, many ended at Southampton. But *Caronia* fares always included a first-class return in any other Cunarder of choice including either of the immensely popular *Queens*. After annual dry docking in December, the *Caronia* often returned to New York in January with a triangular voyage – to Bermuda, Nassau and the likes of Barbados and Kingston before heading north for the beginning of her world cruise.

While the *Caronia* could carry over 900 passengers for her very occasional transatlantic 'positioning' voyages, her cruise capacity was limited to some 600, but in actual fact it rarely ever exceeded 350–400. She had an all-British crew of 600 and so the service ratio was exceptionally high. She had a club-like quality among her passengers and so many tended to come year after year. Some stayed aboard for two and three years at a time while one woman, Clara MacBeth, 'lived' on the ship for a total of fourteen years! She paid Cunard a total of $4 million in pre-inflationary fares!

John Ferguson, today a cruise specialist, served aboard the legendary *Caronia* in the late 1950s.

'I remember the wonderful smells in the early morning of toast and coffee being made in the individual pantries for the cabin breakfasts and which were served on wooden trays,' he recalled.

The *Caronia* had all-British waiters, stewards and stewardesses. The food was excellent, but actually the ship had the worst coffee that ever put to sea. Of the two restaurants, the Balmoral was the much preferred. The other, the Sandringham, was the cabin or second-class dining room when the ship made occasional Atlantic crossings and so you were always a sort of second class citizen!'

Outdoors, the *Caronia* actually had very little deck space and a tiny, little pool, but it didn't matter. Women wore skirts by the pool then. Of course, our passengers were much older. We had nothing close to the entertainments and diversions of today's cruise ships. It was a slower-paced lifestyle then. We took time about the daily activities. There was one event at a time. Perhaps, it was more restful, more tranquil. The Verandah Café, designed as a separate restaurant, was used as a nightclub. The main lounge had huge, old, very heavy furniture and great pillars that actually obstructed the views. Entertainers stayed for an entire cruise, possibly as much as 100 days around the world. There was exhibition dancing, a male or female singer and a comedian. Evenings were, of course, very dressy. And, of course, there were lots of great jewels onboard.

John Ferguson, then just starting a long career with the great Cunard Company, was indeed fortunate to be assigned early on to the splendid *Caronia*.

I was part of Cunard's own cruise staff. In the evenings, I would dance with the ladies and also be an assistant host at cocktail parties. The passenger parties were extraordinary, each of them themed. Once, we made Miss MacBeth the 'ice queen' on a North Cape cruise. Another time, we did the unheard-of – we covered the portrait of Princess Elizabeth in the main lounge for a special group production of *Madame Butterfly*.

John Butt also sailed aboard the *Caronia*.

She was a wonderful ship, perhaps the best in the Cunard fleet in some ways. Her crew was determined by selection. They were all handpicked. The tone onboard was like that of a grand club. One hundred per cent of the passengers did the entire cruise. There were no segment voyages back then. Miss MacBeth hardly went ashore and Helen Howard Jones stayed aboard for more than ten years. The ship was completely green, of course, and this absorbed the sun better. She always consumed far too much fuel and, in the end, she was simply uneconomic.

8973. The Bow, R.M.S. "Queen Mary" Cunard White Star Ltd.) or Southern Railways King George V Graving Dock, Southampton.

Also, her boilers went. She was not viable to repair. On her last cruise [October 1967], there were 600 crew looking after a very empty ship. She had 'slipped her tow' during that voyage, developed water troubles and sailed into a reef. It was all too sad.

The *Caronia* was sold to Greek interests in 1968, refitted slightly as the renamed *Caribia*, but had little success thereafter. Bankrupt and idle, she sat around New York harbour until, while under tow to Taiwanese scrappers in August 1974, she was wrecked on Guam in the Pacific. Broken in three, she was soon broken-up on the spot.

The art deco-style Ocean Terminal was used by Cunard and others. It was opened in 1950, but then, quite sadly, demolished in 1983. (Albert Wilhelmi Collection)

Left Beloved and immensely popular, the *Queen Mary* takes a turn in the King George V Graving Dock at Southampton. (Albert Wilhelmi Collection)

High elegance on the high seas – the first-class main lounge aboard the *Queen Elizabeth*. (Author's Collection)

With forward-facing, wrap-around windows, the first-class observation lounge and bar aboard the *Queen Mary*. (Author's Collection)

The first-class restaurant aboard the *Queen Mary* and where Cunard proudly announced, among many other notations, there were twelve kinds of cereal each morning. (Author's Collection)

The first-class restaurant onboard the *QE*, as she was dubbed, was done in Canadian Maple and sat 850 passengers at one time. (Author's Collection)

Done in softer, lighter styling, the first-class salon onboard the *QE* had a large centre dance floor. (Author's Collection)

The observation lounge and cocktail bar, also aboard the 2,223-passenger *Elizabeth*. (Author's Collection)

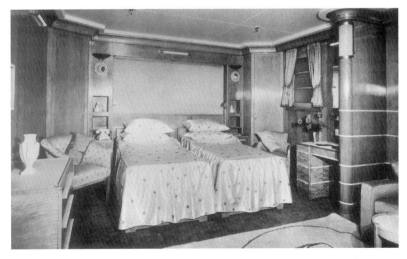

The bedroom of a first-class suite onboard the *QM*. It was priced at $1,200 in the late 1950s for the five-day passage across the Atlantic. (Richard Faber Collection)

There were famous passengers onboard almost all crossings on the Cunard *Queens*. Here, in a view onboard the *Queen Mary* from 1951, we see the Duke and Duchess of Windsor dining in the exclusive Verandah Grill Restaurant with Lord Beaverbrook. (Brenton Jenkins Collection)

Eldest in the post-Second World War Cunard fleet was the 45,647-ton *Aquitania*, completed in 1914 and the last four-stacker. She made Southampton-Halifax sailings in the late 1940s. (Richard Faber Collection)

The sports deck onboard the *Mary* with two of her three distinctive funnels in view. (Richard Faber Collection)

Another veteran, the 19,602-ton *Samaria*, built in 1921, was used in Cunard's Canadian service until scrapped in 1956. (Alex Duncan)

Hail and Farewell! The veteran *Queen Mary* leaves New York for the last time on a late summer's day in September 1967. She had crossed the Atlantic 1,000 times. (Port Authority of New York & New Jersey)

Opposite Settled in gentle retirement, the *Queen Mary* lives on at Long Beach, California, as a museum, hotel and collection of shops and restaurants. In 2006, the cherished ship celebrated the seventieth anniversary of her completion. (Author's Collection)

Above The *Queen Elizabeth* was far less fortunate. After an attempt to make her a hotel and museum at Fort Lauderdale, she was sold to become the Chinese-owned floating university-cruise ship *Seawise University*. Sadly, she burned in Hong Kong harbour in January 1972. (Author's Collection)

The smallest of the pre-war Cunard Canadian liners was the 14,100-ton *Ascania*. Seen here at Halifax, she was retired in late 1956. (Richard Faber Collection)

The tall funnel of the *Franconia*, completed in 1923, photographed during the 623ft-long ship's last visit to New York in the autumn of 1956. Soon afterward, she was broken-up in Scotland. (Richard Faber Collection)

Beginning in 1962, the *Mauretania* was painted overall in Cunard's 'cruising green' and used mostly for cruises. Her days ended soon afterwards, however – she was sold to shipbreakers in Scotland in November 1965. (Cunard Line)

The *Mauretania* of 1939 was, like the *Queen Elizabeth*, considered to be one of the most handsome-looking liners of her time. She is seen here departing from Southampton. (Cunard Line)

During one of her long, luxurious Mediterranean cruises, the *Caronia* spends the day in this poetic scene at Villefranche. (Albert Wilhelmi Collection)

Classic Cunard decor: the *Mauretania*'s first-class main restaurant. (Albert Wilhelmi Collection)

Above Completed in 1930 and used until sold to the breakers in late 1960, the *Britannic* was the last of the White Star Line ships used by Cunard. The name Cunard-White Star, taken on during the merger of the two companies in 1934, was used until 1950, when it reverted simply to Cunard. (Cronican-Arroyo Collection)

Opposite above Said to be the finest cruise ship of her time and one of the most luxurious liners afloat, the 1948-built *Caronia* was Britain's largest post-war liner and the biggest single-stacker to date. (Albert Wilhelmi Collection)

The first-class main lounge onboard the *Caronia*. There is a portrait of the then Princess Elizabeth and the Duke of Edinburgh at the far end. (Cunard Line)

The smoking room onboard the 34,183-ton *Caronia*. (Cunard Line)

On a winter's day, with an ice-filled Hudson River, the 250-passenger, all-first-class *Parthia* rests on the south side of Cunard's Pier 92 at New York. (Cunard Line)

Cunard's only combination passenger-cargo liners, the *Media* – seen here at the Huskisson Dock at Liverpool – and her sister *Parthia* were popular for a time on their nine-day crossings to and from New York. (F. Leonard Jackson Collection)

Intimate luxury: the main lounge aboard the one-class *Parthia*. (Albert Wilhelmi Collection)

Beginning in 1954, Cunard built four brand new 22,000-ton liners especially for their Canadian service – the *Saxonia* (seen here), *Ivernia*, *Carinthia* and *Sylvania*. (Richard Faber Collection)

Contemporary 1950s decor: the tourist-class main lounge aboard the *Saxonia*. (Richard Faber Collection)

Sold to the Sitmar Line in 1968, the *Fairwind* (ex-*Sylvania*) and the *Fairland* (ex-*Carinthia* and soon renamed *Fairsea*) wait at Southampton. With their Cunard days over, they are both soon off to lavish conversions to modern cruise ships. (Cunard Line)

The former *Ivernia*, renamed *Franconia* in 1962, spent her later years as the Soviet *Feodor Shalyapin*. Seen here at Lisbon, she ended her long career in the winter of 2004 when she was broken-up in India. (Luis Miguel Correia Collection)

Framed by a Birkenhead ferry, the *Carinthia* is in mid-Mersey at Liverpool in this very poetic, late afternoon scene. (F. Leonard Jackson Collection)

The *Queen Elizabeth II*, launched in September 1967 and commissioned in May 1968, was the last of the great British-built, British-owned liners of the 1950s and '60s. At 67,000 tons and carrying 1,700 passengers, she was also said to be the very last transatlantic super liner. She was succeeded in 2004, however, by the larger 151,000-ton *Queen Mary II*. The thirty-nine-year-old, long-serving, highly successful *QE2* was retired and sold to owners in Dubai in November 2008. (Alex Duncan)

9

DONALDSON OF GLASGOW

In the spring of 1925, the Donaldson Line ran two larger liners on the North Atlantic, sailing between Glasgow and Montreal. They were twin sisters, built in the same style of those single-stack Cunard liners of the same period, by Fairfield shipyards of Glasgow. The *Athenia* came first, entering service in the spring of 1923; the *Letitia* joined two years later, in the spring of 1923.

On 3 September 1939, the 13,500-ton *Athenia* gained maritime immortality. She became the first sea-going victim of the Second World War. She was sunk by a Nazi U-boat some 200 nautical miles west of the Hebrides. One hundred and twelve were lost. The news was especially horrifying as even the enemy agreed that no action should be taken against unarmed, civilian passenger ships. At best, the Nazi High Command could only deny and then ignore the incident.

The *Letitia* was soon called to duty, first as an armed merchant cruiser, then as a trooper and finally as a hospital ship. With the war ended, in 1946, she was sold outright to the British Ministry of Transport, although retaining Donaldson management. She was renamed *Empire Brent*. A year or so later, she was refitted to become a peacetime troopship, with a pressing need for her to go to India and later to the Far East. Still later, beginning in June 1951 and lasting for seven months, she was converted to an immigrant ship at Glasgow. The troop accommodations came out and were replaced by 1,088 all-third-class berths. She was assigned to the migrant run out to New Zealand. More appropriately, her name was changed to *Captain Cook*.

Captain Harvey Smith served aboard the 538ft-long liner in the early 1950s:

The *Cook* was owned by the British Government, but still managed by Donaldson's. We had segregation onboard: separate sections for males and females. She was quite spartan. Some of the pre-war ambience survived, however. The orchestra gallery remained in the restaurant and several public rooms were in tact with their period furnishings.

We sailed from Glasgow every three months, top heavy with migrants, bound for Wellington via the Panama Canal. Homewards, we travelled empty. We were under the command of Captain James Cook, who had mastered the *Athenia* before the war. The *Captain Cook* was honoured when, in June 1953, we were at the Queen's Coronation Review off Spithead. In 1955, we were used for the Donaldson transatlantic service, making a number of crossings to Montreal.

The *Captain Cook* finished her days in 1960 when she was scrapped at Inverkeithing.

Donaldson also ran a revived transatlantic service, using two converted, former American Victory Class ships, the *Taos Victory* and the *Medina Victory*, which were given to Britain in 1946 and rebuilt as passenger-cargo ships in 1948–49. Renamed *Laurentia* and *Lismoria*, they were fitted with fifty-five all-first-class berths and used on the Glasgow-Montreal run (and to St John, New Brunswick, and Halifax in winter). They endured until late 1966, when they were used briefly as freighters before being sold and as Donaldson was disbanded. The 8,300-ton *Laurentia* was scrapped on Taiwan in the summer of 1967, and the *Lismoria was* broken-up in Spain in the winter of 1967.

Converted to carry fifty-five passengers each, the sisters *Laurentia* and *Lismoria* (seen here) had been Victory Ships, built 1944-45. (Richard Faber Collection)

The 1925-built *Letitia* of the Donaldson Line spent her final years as the immigrant ship *Captain Cook*. (Richard Faber Collection)

10

WEST AFRICA BOUND: ELDER DEMPSTER LINES

In that now long-vanished age of political empires, Britain had links to almost every continent. Ships were, in that pre-jet era, the only connections between motherland and colony. They carried passengers, the ministers and civil servants, as well as cargo, and were often supported by generous contracts from London, especially for the transport of Her Majesty's mails. Certainly, one of the biggest and busiest trades was to Africa. And so, while Union-Castle dominated the run to South Africa and the British India Line to the East Coast, it was the Liverpool-based Elder Dempster Lines that plied the West Coast trade. Their last passenger ship, a rather splendid-looking, yacht-like liner, the 537ft-long *Aureol*, ran that service for well over twenty years, until 1974.

Built in 1951 by one of Scotland's more noted shipbuilders, Alexander Stephen & Sons of Glasgow, the 14,000-ton *Aureol* had space for 353 passengers – 253 in first class, seventy-six in cabin and twenty-four in third. A motorship, she made month-long roundtrips out of Liverpool via Las Palmas in the Canaries to the West African ports of Freetown, Takoradi and Lagos. The late C.M. Squarey, the well-known ship appraiser for Thomas Cook in the 1950s, wrote favourably of her: 'Her white hull with gold band around it, her almost clipper bow, her nicely rounded bridge and her stocky yellow funnel all unite to give the ship a most pleasing profile. My forecast is that many people will reckon that she is the prettiest ship based at Liverpool.'

Sailing for many years with two other Elder Dempster passenger ships, the *Accra* and *Apapa*, decolonization coupled with the rise of airline travel spelled their ends. Elder Dempster was reduced to all freighters by 1974. Initially, the 16-knot *Aureol* was to have been sold to Pakistani buyers, to become a Moslem pilgrim ship, but this never occurred and so she went to the Greeks instead, to oil tanker billionaire John S. Latsis. Registered to one of his Panama-flag subsidiaries, his strong link to Saudi Arabia provided a future for the ship. She served as a moored hotel for oil crews and engineers both at Jeddah and at Rabegh. As the *Marianna VI*, Latsis had another hotel ship in the same Arabian waters. She was the *Margarita L*, the former *Windsor Castle*, another one-time British-African liner.

The 11,644-ton *Accra* and her twin sister *Apapa* were built in 1947–48 for Elder Dempster's run to West Africa. (World Ship Society)

Often likened to be a large, all-white yacht, the 537ft-long *Aureol* – seen here anchored in the Mersey at Liverpool – endured for fifty-two years, being demolished in India in 2003. (F. Leonard Jackson Collection)

11

ELLERMAN: 'YACHTS' TO SOUTH AFRICA

In the spring of 1990, the London-based Ellerman Lines – then merged into a cargo operation with Cunard, but later sold to P&O – announced that it was restoring passenger service, although a limited one, between England and South Africa. Twelve berths had been added to at least one of their big containerships, the 58,000-ton *City of Durban*. She ran a regular service between Southampton, Capetown and Durban. The passenger service marked a resumption of a link that, in fact, ended for Ellerman some twenty years before, in 1971. Then, their last passenger ships were retired. This revived service not only marked a reversal in history, but was another sign of the renewed interest at the time in passenger service aboard cargo ships. Several other firms restored limited passenger operations as well.

Well known and very popular in British travel circles in particular, the last Ellerman passenger ships were a superb quartet and were named *City of Port Elizabeth*, *City of Exeter*, *City of York* and *City of Durban*, built in 1952–54. While actually classed as combination passenger-cargo ships (at 13,300 gross tons each), their passenger quarters, with only 107 all-first-class berths, were so comfortable and so well served that these ships were often thought of as being like large yachts. They were often booked well in advance and, in fact, were even more

Superb combination passenger-cargo liners Ellerman's *City of York* and her three sisters carried up to 107 passengers in all-first-class accommodations. (Alex Duncan)

The same ship, but rebuilt as the Greek-owned *Mediterranean Sky,* is seen here in a view dated 24 October 1984, in off-season lay-up in Eleusis Bay. (Steffen Weirauch Collection)

End of the line: the *Mediterranean Sea* (ex-*City of Exeter*) being demolished at Aliaga in Turkey in July 1999. (Selim San)

popular than first class on the larger, competitive Union-Castle liners, which plied the same South African route.

Captain Ian Taylor, retired and living in the English countryside, served in these ships and recalled them in a November 1990 interview. 'Yes, indeed, these ships were like big yachts,' he noted enthusiastically.

They were magnificent in every way. And the service ratio was extraordinary. We had sixty-nine Calcutta stewards plus eight extra European staff to look after the hundred or so passengers. Many were loyalists and others came annually. They tended to be English and older, often from fifty to seventy. Usually, they were bound for South African holidays, often an escape from the dreary English winters, on family visits and for safaris. Others made the complete roundtrip, a sort of cruise. London to London was seven weeks. It would take thirteen days just to sail from London to Capetown and with only a brief refuelling stop in the Canaries.

But the South African trade was not their only passenger business according to Captain Taylor.

We also offered a week-long 'mini cruise' in North European waters. It proved very, very popular. Many perspective travellers used these trips before booking a full African voyage. After unloading our inbound cargo at London, we would go up the English East Coast to Newcastle or Middlesbrough, to load machinery and iron products, and then sail across the North Sea to Hamburg, Rotterdam and Antwerp before returning to London, where we would reload for the outbound voyage.

Very popular to the very end, these City liners, as they were often dubbed, began to face stiffer competition in the late 1960s. Mostly, their all-important cargos went over to far larger and faster containerships. 'It was quite traumatic to lose this *City of Durban* class, but they needed huge and expensive refits as well by this time,' concluded Captain Taylor. 'They had lots of loyal and regular passengers to the end, but this wasn't quite enough.'

The *City of York* made the last Ellerman Lines passenger sailing in June 1971, or so everyone thought. The revival of that twelve-passenger container ship service was encouraging. Of the earlier ships, they were sold to Greek buyers, the Karageorgis Lines. All four were to be converted to high-standard ferries, but then plans were reduced to two ships. The *City of Durban*, which became the *Mediterranean Dolphin*, was scrapped in 1974, soon after her sale to the Greeks. The *City of Port Elizabeth* changed to *Mediterranean Island*, but was laid-up until 1980 and then scrapped. The other two sisters were extensively rebuilt: the *City of Exeter* became the *Mediterranean Sea*, listed at 16,384 tons and with space for 895 passengers and 350 cars. The *City of York* changed to *Mediterranean Sky*. Used mostly in Adriatic and Aegean services, they were also used for periodic cruises, did Libyan charters and even served as an accommodation ship in Cuba. The *Mediterranean Sea* (ex-*City of Exeter*) sailed as the *Alice* in her final years before being scrapped in Turkey in the summer of 1999; the *Mediterranean Sky* (ex-*City of York*) sank at her moorings in Eleusis Bay in November 2002.

12

THE HONEYMOON SHIPS: FURNESS-BERMUDA LINE

'She was one of the most popular liners ever to sail,' stated the late Everett Viez, a top ocean liner traveller and collector who began in the late 1920s. He made trips on over 100 different passenger ships. 'There were few ships better than the *Queen of Bermuda*. She was a true favourite of mine,' he told me in one of his last interviews in the late 1990s.

> She had more luxury about her than many transatlantic liners. The service was impeccable and the food top-notch. She was also an immaculate ship. She was first class in every way. She ran immensely popular six-day cruises between New York and Bermuda. In fact, the Bermuda run was a 'gold mine' for her British owners.

Begun in 1919 and highlighted in the 1930s by the creation of two, quite luxurious, near-sisters, the *Monarch of Bermuda* (1931) and the *Queen of Bermuda* (1933), the Company was anxious to resume their cruise-like operations soon after the Second World War. The *Monarch of Bermuda* burned out during her post-war refit in 1947 and, while thought to be good only for the scrappers, she was, in fact, sold to the British Government and rebuilt as the comparatively austere Australian immigrant ship *New Australia*. She was managed, however, by Shaw Savill for her low-fare, all-tourist-class services. While the *Queen of Bermuda* resumed luxury service in February 1949, Furness-Bermuda built a brand new replacement ship, the 13,600-ton *Ocean Monarch*, which was commissioned in the spring of 1951. The two ships were fine partners, maintaining the weekly Bermuda service from New York as well as offering periodic cruises – to Eastern Canada in the summer and deep into the Caribbean in high winter.

'Those six-day cruises between New York and Bermuda were the ideal family vacation as well as a honeymoon special,' said Desmond Kirkpatrick, who sailed as an assistant purser aboard the 516ft-long *Ocean Monarch* in the early 1960s.

Of course, we had lots of families during the school holidays in high summer. We also had many one-way passengers, some of which stayed on the Island and then flew home. The ships went either to St George or Hamilton.

Even if it was only a six-day cruise, there were big crowds on sailing day at 3 p.m. on Saturday afternoons at Pier 95, New York. There were these elaborate parties before sailing with family and friends coming aboard. The six-day voyage was like a mini Atlantic crossing and so it was seen as a significant trip. Primarily, we had British deck and engine crew as well as some Bermudians, some of which had been with Furness for years. We would always make a trip back to the UK each year for refit and overhaul, but the Bermudians did not go on these.

The *Ocean Monarch* was smaller, a friendly cruise ship. She carried 400 or so passengers and so was quite yacht-like. In winter, however, she was not the friendliest sea boat. There were no stabilizers, just Flume tanks. Once I was thrown out of my bunk. Another dramatic moment was at Christmas Eve, during a Holiday cruise to Bermuda as well as Nassau, there was a fire in the funnel and then it flashed down to the boilers. We had been in a nasty rain squall and the rain water seeped into the funnel, which short-circuited some wiring and then set some soot on fire. Once we returned to New York, the next cruise was cancelled and we went straight over to the Bethlehem Steel shipyard in Hoboken for repairs. For our annual UK refits, we crossed the Atlantic and then spent a month at Belfast or Birkenhead or sometimes Newcastle.

The *Ocean Monarch* was caught at New York during the Big Blackout of November 1965. Members of CBS-TV news, housed in a nearby building, saw us and thought of us, with power, as 'a sea of light in an ocean of darkness'. They called us and asked if we could house their news staff overnight. So, we had to prepare cabins in a hurry. I did the berthing. And we provided urns of coffee and tea, and prepared platters of sandwiches. In the morning, there was a buffet breakfast. Walter Cronkite, the famed newscaster, later visited the ship, interviewed the captain and donated two large colour televisions to the ship, one for the crew mess and the other for the officers' mess.

Above Rebuilt in 1961–62, the legendary *Queen of Bermuda* was restyled with a single funnel. Previously, she had three funnels and, for a time during the Second World War, two funnels. (Author's Collection)

Left Outbound on her maiden voyage from New York to Bermuda, the 13,654-ton, 440-passenger *Ocean Monarch* was then called 'the largest cruise ship in the world'. (Cronican-Arroyo Collection)

While the 22,500-ton *Queen of Bermuda* was extensively refitted and modernised in 1961–62 (changing from three funnels to a single one in the process), newly enacted American maritime safety standards set for 1968 prompted Furness to retire both ships – the *Queen of Bermuda* went to scrappers at Faslane in Scotland in December 1966 while the *Ocean Monarch* was retired in September 1966 and then sold the following June to Bulgarian buyers, who used her as the cruise ship *Varna*. Laid-up in 1974–79 due to fuel oil price increases, she was sold to Greek buyers in 1979 and became the *Riviera*, but for revived cruising that never materialised. Next, she was to become the *Venus* for a return to New York-Bermuda service, but this failed to materialise as well. She was, however, renamed *Reina Del Mar* in 1981 for projected European cruising with mostly British passengers, but was destroyed by fire while undergoing a refit at Perama in Greece on 28 May 1981. Soon afterward, she capsized and was declared a total loss.

Right Furness also ran, in their Furness Warren Line division, a North Atlantic service between Liverpool, St John's on Newfoundland, Halifax and Boston until 1961. The 7,400-ton sisters *Newfoundland* (shown here) and *Nova Scotia*, built in 1947–48, carried 154 passengers in first and tourist class quarters. Sold to become the Pacific-based *Francis Drake* and *George Anson* in 1962, they were both scrapped in 1971. (Alex Duncan)

Above A very popular team seen here in the 1950s at Hamilton, Bermuda – the *Ocean Monarch* on the left, the *Queen of Bermuda* on the right. (Cronican-Arroyo Collection)

13

FYFFES AND 'BANANA BOATS'

A trip on a 'banana boat' conjures up all sorts of romantic, seagoing notions – a long, lazy voyage, tropic nights and visits to palm tree-lined ports. There were once dozens of passenger-carrying banana boats, ships usually fitted with quarters from twelve or 100 or so passengers. Today, a few still remain. But two of the largest in the last fifty years were the near-sisters *Golfito* and *Camito*. And while not especially well known outside Britain, they ran a very popular service in their day for the Fyffes Line or Elder & Fyffes Ltd. Expectedly, bananas were their primary business and this was perhaps best exemplified by a familiar but unofficial staff slogan: 'Every banana is a guest, every passenger is a pest!'

The *Golfito* and *Camito* were quite comfortable ships. Each had quarters for about 100 passengers, all first class. There were three decks with cabins, public rooms and open-air deck spaces. All of this was positioned between four large cargo holds, two forward and two aft. These could handle as many as 140,000 stems (or 1,750 tons) of bananas. Their main trade was to take general cargo outwards and then return with bananas in their refrigerated compartments on the homebound trips.

'They were very popular little passenger ships,' remembered James Moran, who served aboard both ships as a restaurant waiter.

Their overall style was adequate, but simple. The main lounge, for example, was straight out of an Agatha Christie film. There was a round wooden pool on the deck that was built by the crew. I especially recall the after-dinner fare: the Chief Purser calling out bingo as everyone sat around sipping pink gins. Very occasionally, there might be a film using a portable projector and makeshift screen. Of course, at four every afternoon, we had a high tea.

'The ships were routed on four to five-week long voyages from Southampton or Avonmouth and then sailed across to Barbados, Trinidad and then to as many as five ports on Jamaica – Kingston, Port Antonio, Montego Bay, Oracabessa and Bowdin. We used to load the bananas all through the night when it was much cooler and so comes the well known song by Mr Harry Belafonte: 'Mr Tallyman daylight comes and I want to go home!

We tended to carry upper-class British passengers back then. We had the plantation owners, government officials, colonial people and, of course, the winter holiday crowd. We also carried lots of businessmen, remembering that much of the Caribbean was then British colonial territory. Particularly, I remember carrying the Mount Gay twins, two wonderfully eccentric women, and Princess Alice, the last of Queen Victoria's grandchildren. She was then the Chancellor of the University of the West Indies in Kingston and travelled with us at least once a year. A very delightful, totally undemanding lady and a great aunt to Queen Elizabeth II. I do recall, however, that she and her lady-in-waiting sat at opposite tables in the dining room. We also had a rather legendary doctor onboard. He always kept a pickled appendix on his desk and, no matter what the ailment, gave everyone a portion of rum in a small medicine bottle.

While the Fyffes Line also maintained a fleet of passenger-carrying freighters, these two 8,700-ton ships survived until the mid-'70s. By then, they had lost much of their earlier clientele to speedier jets, were growing older themselves and generally had become less efficient and therefore less profitable. Both finished their days at the scrapyards and so ended the last of the big, British 'banana boats'.

Handsome ships, the near-sisters *Golfito* (built in 1949 and shown here) and *Camito* carried a little more than 100 passengers each on the UK-Caribbean run. They were, rather expectedly, very popular in winter. (Luis Miguel Correia Collection)

14

'NICE SHIPS' - THE GLEN LINE

In the 1950s, the London/Liverpool-based Glen Line had a rather unusual, even eccentric group of what were then large freighters that carried sixteen to eighteen passengers each. Most actual freighters limited the maximum to twelve. The main, if not the only reason for this, was that more than twelve passengers required a passenger certificate from the Ministry of Transport in London and the addition of an onboard doctor or well-qualified medical officer. Therefore, going above the twelve passengers called for added standards and cost extra money. And so, for these Glen Line ships, why not, say, thirty, fifty, even seventy-five passengers? An eclectic group in other ways, they sailed on the long-haul Europe-Far East run until the 1960s.

At approximately 9,000 tons, the first group – named *Breconshire*, *Glenartney*, *Glenearn*, *Glengyle* and *Glenorchy* – were built in Scotland between 1938 and 1941. The *Denbighshire* was completed at Amsterdam in 1938 while the *Glengarry* was constructed at Copenhagen in 1940. A last member, the 507ft-long *Glenroy*, was built at Greenock in 1938. Most of them had diverse histories, which included varied wartime uses and changes in names. Each was subsequently scrapped in either Taiwan or Japan from 1967 until 1971.

C.M. Squarey wrote of his visit to the smart-looking *Glenartney* in June 1953. 'There is about the passenger quarters in this ship quite a remarkable sense of spaciousness,' he noted.

There is nothing ostentatious in her interior decoration, but instead what impressed me was the air of quiet dignity that pervades the ship. There is a feeling that she comes from a line of aristocrats. She has a fine lounge spanning the ship, and a dining saloon on the deck below of similar proportions. Those who serve and administer to the passenger needs are all Chinese – and first rate at their job too.

The cabins are all good rooms, though I think fitted carpets would have added just a little certain something to their appearance. It is the practice of the Line not to allocate actual room numbers until embarkation time, the argument for this system being that the rooms are all much on a par with each other. The policy of the Glen Line towards passengers is, 'We like to carry nice passengers in nice surroundings!' I should say that the *Glenartney* fulfils that policy admirably.

These ships, reduced in their final years to twelve-passenger freighters, were scrapped in the Far East between 1966 and 1972.

Glen Line's *Denbighshire*, built at Amsterdam in 1938, carried up to eighteen one-class passengers on the UK-Far East run. At the end of her days in 1968, she became the *Sarpedon* for China Mutual Steam Navigation before going to the breakers a year later. (Gillespie-Faber Collection)

Another combo ship with eighteen passenger berths, the *Glenorchy* had been built in 1941 as Blue Funnel's *Priam*, a name in which she is seen here in a rare view at Pier 14 in Lower Manhattan in 1946. She was transferred over to the Glen Line in 1948 and then changed names. (Richard Faber Collection)

HENDERSON'S TO BURMA

Glasgow-based P. Henderson & Co. was another well-established British shipping line, one dating from 1840. Like the Bibby Line, they had strong interests in the very lucrative Burmese trades. They came under Elder Dempster control in 1952 and by the end of that decade had two remaining passenger-cargo ships, the 7,000-ton, seventy-six-passenger *Prome* and her sister, the *Salween*. They sailed in regular service from Liverpool to Port Said, Port Sudan, Aden, Colombo and Rangoon. Henderson survived as an independent company until 1962, when these two ships were retired and scrapped – the *Prome* being broken-up that year in Belgium and the *Salween* at Hong Kong.

The Henderson Line came under Elder Dempster management in 1952 and had two passenger ships, the *Prome* and *Salween* (seen here), on the Liverpool-Suez-Rangoon run. Built in the late 1930s, these 7,000-tonners carried some seventy-five passengers each in all-first-class accommodations. (Alex Duncan)

NEW ZEALAND SHIPPING CO.

'If I likened that pair of pre-war, twin-stackers, the *Rangitiki* and *Rangitata*, to the fine life in a good country house, I think that the new *Rangitoto* [and her sistership *Rangitane*] has many of the better features of a good country club,' said passenger ship chronicler C.M. Squarey in the summer of 1949. He and 180 or so other guests had just made a short, pre-maiden voyage cruise in that very large combo liner from her Clydeside birthplace in Scotland down to the Thames, to the London Docks.

After the Second World War, the New Zealand Shipping Co. had only two very suitable passenger ships, the aforementioned *Rangitiki* and *Rangitata*, both built in 1929, for its future needs on the long-distance England-New Zealand via Panama trade. A third survivor, the aging, 1923-built *Rimutaka*, was soon sold off. And so, three of the mightiest combination passenger-cargo liners ever built were ordered – a set of sisters and then one slightly smaller ship.

The *Rangitoto* and *Rangitata* weighed in at just under 22,000 tons and measured 609ft in length. They had diesels and could make 16½ knots at maximum speed. The *Ruahine* was slightly smaller, at 17,800 tons. Also, between 1962–64, the Company operated Cunard's former *Parthia*, a 13,600-tonner, built in 1948, that sailed as the *Remuera*. They were routed from London to Curacao, the Panama Canal, Tahiti, Wellington and Auckland. Along with large quantities of cargo (British-manufactured goods going outwards and mostly meat and wool coming home), the sisters *Rangitane* and *Rangitoto* were fitted with accommodation for 436 one-class passengers, and the *Ruahine* for 267 travellers. Wrote Mr Squarey:

Nothing quite like it had been attempted before. As many as 400 people travelling on a one-class only basis, paying fares ranging from £77 to 178 – a difference of £101. It is an enterprising experiment and certainly deserves to reap fruits of success. These are democratic times, and this democratic venture in new living applied on the high seas will be watched with high interest.

Squarey was quite impressed with the powerful, 21-knot *Rangitoto* and her passenger quarters.

The main lounge, with its really large windows (a feature throughout the ship), with its exceptional height and its gay, but not gaudy furnishings, is a room of much charm. The writing and reading rooms are most satisfying in their decoration and layout – the writing desks, for example, are sensibly located, and one is spared the irksome ordeal of looking up from one's notepaper to be greeted by some pen-chewing passenger sitting opposite, scratching for news in his letter. Then comes the well-mirrored dance room out which leads to the Verandah Café, which adjoins the excellent deck area running the full beam of the ship at the stern and of which is a pleasant swimming pool. Deck game facilities on the Boat Deck are very good. A nice cinema occupies the starboard side amidships. One thought, however, that goes through my mind is that perhaps the cinema space might be more effectively used as a smoking room. True, there is a Smoking Room on C Deck, but because it is relatively so small, it seems to me to have all the makings of that most excellent institution, 'the village pub'.

Ruahine is a Maori word meaning 'old woman'. It is also the name chosen for the third of these NZSCO combo liners. Some 4,000 tons smaller, she is a result of the Company's experiences and operating results with the two previous ships. She was, however, not exactly a compressed edition of the originals, for certain features were changed. She won praises on her own, however.

'The *Ruahine* emerges as a well-thought-out ship, well furnished, pleasantly decorated – in one word, she is a decent ship,' noted C.M. Squarey.

I think, however, that with a full load, she will find herself hard-pressed for space in the public rooms when weather confines everyone inboard. Also, in the four-berth cabins, passengers may find the wardrobe and drawer space on

During one of the Port of London's 'River & Docks' cruises, passengers see a fine array of shipping that includes NZSCO's *Rangitiki*. (S.W. Rawlings Collection)

the short side for stowing their effects. But they must remember that this ship does not profess to provide first class amenities. She is a 'happy ship'. I reached the conclusion partly on a choice remark made to one of the stewards. Asked what had been his last ship, he replied that he had been in another trade for one voyage, but had come back to NZSCO because they have 'decent ships and you are treated decently'.

New Zealander John Draffin served in the *Ruahine* in the early 1960s as a junior assistant purser. 'We had general cargo and lots of migrants going outbound,' he remembered.

Homebound, we had New Zealanders as tourists and earlier migrants going back to the UK to visit their families. Homeward, nearly all of the 8,000 tons of total cargo was frozen lamb, but we also carried some wool and casin, a milk by-product used in making glue. It was ten days from London to Curacao, then two days to Panama, twelve to Tahiti and eight to Auckland. We would have six weeks in New Zealand loading lamb. At the other end, at London, we would have four weeks in the Royal Albert Docks.

There was no air-conditioning on the *Ruahine*, except in the restaurant and purser's office. All entertainment was organized by the passengers themselves and most of it was done on deck. It seemed that every last passenger participated as well. We did have records for dancing in the lounge. New

Zealand Shipping was a subsidiary of P&O and a sister company to Federal Steam Navigation.

This passenger service was phased-out in 1969. The *Rangitoto* actually closed out NZSCO's ninety-seven-year-old passenger service in July 1969. She was then sold to Mr C.Y. Tung's fast-growing fleet, joining his Orient Overseas Line division as the *Oriental Carnaval*. She was refitted for 300 all-first-class passengers and used in around-the-world service until laid-up in 1975 and then scrapped on Taiwan a year later. The *Rangitane* was withdrawn in May 1968 and then sold to Greek intermediate buyers, renamed *Jan* and sent on a final voyage to Taiwan for scrapping. The scrapping was delayed, however, and she was sold instead, also to Orient Overseas Line. She was refitted for 300 all-first-class passengers as the *Oriental Esmeralda* and used in around the world service. Transferred in 1974 to Far East and Central American passenger services, she was scrapped at Kaohsiung in Taiwan in 1976. The *Ruahine* also went to C.Y. Tung, becoming the *Oriental Rio* in 1968. She was later scrapped, also in Taiwan, in 1974. The *Remuera*, ex-*Parthia*, was quite unsuccessful. She joined NZSCO in 1962, but was sold two years, becoming *Aramac* for the Sydney-based Eastern & Australian Steamship Co. Ltd. She served in the Pacific until broken-up in Taiwan in 1970.

New additions for NZSCO: the 21,800-ton sisters *Rangitoto* and *Rangitane* (shown here) were among the largest combination passenger-cargo liners in the world. Each carried 436 one-class passengers on the long run out to New Zealand. (Richard Faber Collection)

Slightly smaller than the previous pair, the 17,851-ton *Ruahine*, commissioned in 1951, had space for 267 passengers. (Albert Wilhelmi Collection)

Cunard's 13,600-ton *Parthia* was taken over in 1961 and refitted as the *Remuera*. Withdrawn within two years, however, she became the *Aramac* (as seen here) for Australia-Far East service. (Luis Miguel Correia Collection)

17

QUEENS OF THE SEA: PACIFIC STEAM NAVIGATION

When the Pacific Steam Navigation Co. Ltd of Liverpool decided to replace their aged, but very popular *Reina Del Pacifico* (built in 1931 and 17,800 tons) in the mid-'50s, they returned to the same shipbuilders, the noted Harland & Wolff Company at Belfast. While this replacement would be a modern vessel, including such amenities as full air-conditioning and far more private plumbing in her passenger cabins, she would still have a substantial cargo capacity (five holds in all) and the traditional three classes (207 in first class, 216 in cabin class and 343 in tourist class) similar to her predecessor. Launched on 7 June 1955 as the *Reina Del Mar*, the 'Queen of the Sea', she was Pacific Steam's new flagship – and ultimately their final liner.

The routing to the West Coast of South America via the Panama Canal was one of the most extensive for any British passenger ship. It was a trade then, in the 1950s, still supported by large numbers of port-to-port and interport passengers, sea travellers who might remain aboard the ship for weeks or for as little as two or three nights. After departing from the Liverpool Docks, she would call briefly at La Rochelle in France and then Santander and Corunna in Spain before crossing the mid-Atlantic to Bermuda, Nassau, Havana, Kingston, La Guaira, Curacao, Cartagena, Cristobal and then the Panama Canal, La Libertad, Callao, Arica, Antofagasta and finally a turnaround at Valparaiso in Chile. There would be well-to-do Latin Americans and diplomats in first class, the businessmen and trade merchants in cabin class (the equivalent of today's airline club classes) and then the budget tourists, students and immigrants in tourist class.

A strikingly handsome ship, painted overall in white and offset by a single, tapered, all-yellow funnel, she had a forward mast only. All rigging was therefore attached to the funnel. There were three cargo holds forward, worked by six booms, and two aft, which were handled by four booms. The first-class quarters were exceptionally comfortable and luxurious, and included two suites deluxe and all other cabins with private bathrooms. Cabin class, slightly smaller and less ornate, included one to four berth rooms. In tourist class, cabins were one to six berth. Unfortunately, the 601ft-long *Reina Del Mar* had about five years of profitable service. Like so many other passenger firms, her owners could not have envisioned the swift, almost merciless invasion of jet aircraft. In a very short time, months in fact, almost all of the *Reina Del Mar*'s South American passengers had deserted her in favour of airline travel.

While there were reports that the liner would be retired from British-flag service and then sold off to the then ever-growing Chandris Lines of Greece, she was quite fortunate in securing an extensive charter that began in 1963. Travel entrepreneur Max Wilson's Travel Savings Association, the TSA, was then well into expansion. Supported by the likes of Canadian Pacific and Union Castle, Wilson's concept was to offer inexpensive 'fun in the sun' cruise voyages. He had already chartered such ships as P&O's *Strathmore* and *Stratheden*, and Canadian Pacific's *Empress of Britain* and *Empress of England*. To him, the *Reina Del Mar* seemed the ideal year-round cruise ship.

Once retired from three-class South American service, she was sent to Belfast and structurally rebuilt for full-time cruising. A new, highly successful and extremely popular life would then begin for the *Reina Del Mar*. John Havers, an ardent ocean liner historian and former staff member with Union Castle, recalled her rather elaborate transformation. 'Here was a three-class liner successfully converted for one-class cruising. Her capacity was increased from 766 to 1,047 berths by extending the number of beds and bunks in some original cabins and then adding 135 new staterooms, which were built in the former cargo spaces.'

While the *Reina Del Mar* made some sailings for Mr Wilson, including a maiden crossing to New York for the 1964 World's Fair, his TSA operations soon fell on hard times. Among other problems, the likes of Union-Castle resented his success with low-fare British cruising. The British & Commonwealth Shipping Co., the owners of

Union-Castle, were, in fact, the managers of the *Reina Del Mar* also. As the TSA fell into deeper financial trouble, British & Commonwealth gradually became its sole stockholder. Eventually, TSA was dissolved and the ship's operations transferred to Union-Castle's passenger department. The onboard standards, if not quite as crisp and luxuriant as those in first class on the big mailships on the Cape run, were improved and brought into conformity with Union-Castle's overall image. By November 1964, the *Reina Del Mar*, while still actually owned by Pacific Steam Navigation, a part of the large Furness Withy Group and which included the rival Royal Mail Lines' passenger fleet, was leased to Union-Castle and repainted in their colours. (It was not until as late as September 1973, quite close to the ship's retirement in fact, that Union-Castle bought her outright. This then reflected Furness Withy's decision, made in the early 1970s, to phase-out its remaining passenger interests, which included Royal Mail Lines' cruising program with the highly reputed *Andes* and no less than six liners from another sister company, the Shaw Savill Line.)

Thousands cruised on the *Reina Del Mar* each year. From April through October, she sailed from Southampton to the Canaries, West Africa, the Mediterranean and to Scandinavia; for the remaining months, following low-fare, all-one class 'positioning trips' between Southampton and the South African Cape, she cruised from Capetown on voyages to the Indian Ocean and even across to the East Coast of South America.

Although laid-up at Southampton for six weeks, in the spring of 1966, during the devastating British Seamen's Strike, she was perhaps hardest hit in 1973 when the cost of fuel oil dramatically jumped from $35 to $95 per ton. While still often filled to the very last upper berth and still highly regarded by the British travelling public, she was suddenly – and like so many other, older liners – unable to earn her keep. Besides, just as Union-Castle decided to phase-out its last remaining mailships to South Africa (which was to be finalised by the autumn of 1977), the management reluctantly had to include the *Reina Del Mar* as well. In fact, the Company decided to end passenger operations altogether.

The 1974 season was to be the *Reina Del Mar*'s last. Decommissioned in April of the following year, she was laid-up briefly in Cornwall's River Fal awaiting her fate. There were rumours that she would be converted to a permanently moored youth hostel at the Royal Albert Dock in London. The Greeks, Italians and even the Soviets had a look over her, but it was a particularly tense time for aging, fuel-hungry passenger ships. Therefore, she was one of a half-dozen British liners that were sold prematurely at the time to Taiwanese breakers. She reached Kaohsiung on 30 July 1975, and then sat untouched for several months before being broken-up the following winter.

A classic liner and noted motorship of the 1930s, the 17,707-ton *Reina Del Pacifico* plied the Liverpool-Caribbean-West Coast of South America run until retired and then scrapped in Wales in 1958. (Albert Wilhelmi Collection)

The 601ft-long *Reina Del Mar* passes through the Panama Canal on one of her seventy-day roundtrip voyages to the West Coast of South of America. (Albert Wilhelmi Collection)

The 20,334-ton, three-class *Reina Del Mar* is seen taking on passengers at the Princes Landing Stage at Liverpool. (F. Leonard Jackson Collection)

18

TO ALL THE SEVEN SEAS: P&O-ORIENT LINES

Soon after the Second World War, what proved to the last, great, long-distance passenger ship services began to reopen. Apart from the more specialised, highly reputed and heavily documented North Atlantic trade, these long-distance routes spanned the globe – on extended voyages that went out to the likes of South America, South Africa, the Middle East, Australia and the Orient. Until the advent of aircraft, these ships, multi-class vessels, were assured a steady flow of clientele. And most of them carried cargo as well and not simply the express goods on the big transatlantic ships, but more varied products such as manufactured goods, automobiles, machinery, railway equipment and then, in reverse, the localised cargos such as gold, meat, wool, spices, tea and rubber. These ships, often large combination passenger-cargo ships, were indeed the very last of their kind.

The P&O Lines, known also as the P&O-Orient Lines from 1960 until 1966 after its full merger with its long-time rival, the Orient Line, had the biggest and most important long-distance liner fleet in the post-war era. In fact, in 1960, P&O-Orient had the largest liner fleet anywhere in the world. P&O was, from the late 1940s, best known for its service out to Australia, to Fremantle, Melbourne and Sydney. Their well-known Indian service, mostly to Bombay, declined considerably after 1945, a result in great part to India's changed political status. Alternately, the Australian run was in a boom phase for some twenty-five years, until the late 1960s, with tourists, government officials, merchants and businessmen, but mostly outward migrants. The specially promoted fare-assistance program, allowing Britons to resettle 'Down Under' with passage fares as low as £10, kept P&O as well as many other lines filled to the very last upper bunk. One P&O captain later recalled, 'We were often so overcrowded, even in the mid-1960s, that we had to place some of the migrants in first class cabins.'

'But we still had some strong links to India after the Second World War,' added Captain Denis Scott-Mason.

We still had the tea planters and the civil servants who ran India, and who went out for considerable periods of time. They always went home to Britain for their leaves. And, of course, their wives and families travelled with them by sea. Often, they were a very elite group of people. And, of course, you got to know them and know their favourite ships.

Captain Scott-Mason also served aboard some of P&O's 'less fancy' migrant ships of the late 1940s and '50s.

After the war, some of our older ships were converted to carry migrants only. There were no full fare-paying passengers as such. One of these ships was the *Ranchi*. We carried about 900 migrants from Britain to Australia in her. These voyages were completely subsidized by the Australian Government and so P&O made a nice profit. I remember one voyage when we had virtually all Irish migrants going out to Melbourne and Sydney. They were, shall we say, a fairly rough bunch. They were tense – cutting off their roots and so they were sceptical about the future. They didn't know what they were going to. Some of them didn't even know which city in Australia they would end up in. Some of that was decided during the six-week voyage. Some would go to hostels until they established themselves and found jobs and then got their own homes. Some of them actually lived in hostels for years.

These migrants were going to a totally unknown world. Most of them knew very little about Australia and the Australian way of life. They knew very little about the climate, the people or even what sort of life they would lead once there. When we sailed from Tilbury on these voyages, there were very few family members or friends on the quayside. The farewells had been made at home. The migrants came down by train to the ship. So it wasn't actually a very fond farewell at the ship and as they left British soil, sometimes forever. And the voyages themselves could be quite unpleasant. I recall one trip on the old *Ranchi*. Her engines were no longer reliable. Somewhere, soon after we left Port Said and entered the Canal, we broke down completely. We were immovable. We had to drop anchor in the Canal and tie-up alongside the bank. No ship could go north or south. I believe

Veteran, pre-Second World War P&O liners that endured into the 1950s included the 20,800-ton sisters *Maloja* and *Mooltan* (seen here), which dated from 1923. They were used, however, purely as one-class migrant ships on the UK-Australia run. (Young & Sawyer Collection)

Another older liner, the 15,200-ton *Chitral*, commissioned in 1925, was restored after the war and sailed until 1953 on the Australian migrant trade. (Gillespie-Faber Collection)

The 14,280-ton sisters *Corfu* and *Carthage*, dating from 1931, looked after P&O's London-Far East passenger run. (P&O)

we held up a record number of ships, eighty-two in all, until we were finally towed out of the Canal and into Suez Bay. And that was a voyage with a full load of 900 migrants on that non-air conditioned ship. They weren't happy.

Of course, P&O also catered to a first-class clientele on the Australian run. 'I remember one well-known family from southern Australia,' remembered Captain Scott-Mason:

They loved our *Arcadia*. They had special furniture built to order to fit in several of her deluxe cabins. On their annual pilgrimages to and from Britain, they had it installed in these rooms for their personal use. When they left the ship, it was removed and stored below. And they always travelled at the right time of the year. They arrived in Britain at the beginning of the summer, so they had the best of the weather, and then left in early autumn, to return to Australia in summer. P&O also had a large business of young Australians going up to Britain and continental Europe. They were great fun. The whole of the tourist class sections would be youngsters. I remember one homeward trip in the *Himalaya* when we had only twelve passengers in first class and a full load, about 450, in tourist. There were many empty cabins and acres of the deck space in first class on that trip while the young Australians were packed like sardines at the back end of the ship.

In response to substantial Second World War losses and then the foresight of very profitable days ahead, both the P&O and the Orient lines embarked, soon after 1945, on one of the biggest liner rebuilding

programs of all time. No less than seven major liners, many in the 28-29,000-ton category, were created between 1948 and 1954. The Orient Line added a succession of three, rather similar ships – the 1,545-passenger *Orcades* in 1948, the *Oronsay* in 1951 and then the *Orsova* in 1954. Each was quite distinctive in grouping its funnel and mast (there was no mast whatsoever, in fact, aboard the *Orsova*) high atop the bridge and wheelhouse section and also closer to a midships position. They were among the most modern-looking liners of their time. The P&O Lines, having had great success with their five Strath liners from the 1930s, copied their basic design and arrangements, and then used them with some refinements in the 27,900-ton, 1,519-passenger *Himalaya* of 1949, the *Chusan* of 1950 and finally a pair of near-sisters, the *Arcadia* and *Iberia* of 1954.

These post-war P&O-Orient liners were merged with nine survivors from before the war – the *Orontes* and *Orion* of the Orient Line and the *Corfu*, *Carthage*, *Strathaird*, *Stratnaver*, *Strathmore*, *Stratheden* and *Canton* of P&O. Together, they could easily provide weekly services out of London, via the Mediterranean, Suez, Aden and Ceylon, to Australia. In addition, there was a Far Eastern service, also from London, which passed through Suez as well and then continued to South-East Asia and northward in the Far East as far as Japan. P&O expanded in the 1950s to a worldwide operation – sailing to the North American West Coast and sometimes using the Panama Canal route as an alternative.

Above Thirty years old, the *Corfu* waits off Osaka in May 1961 for handing over to Japanese scrappers. (Hisashi Noma Collection)

Opposite above At Southampton, the classic-looking *Strathnaver* is being handled by tugs with the troopship *Empire Windrush* (in the background on the left) and the larger *Orcades* (docked at the right). (P&O)

Opposite below, left Dating from 1932, the 664ft-long *Strathaird* goes off in this view to Hong Kong breakers in July 1961. (Steffen Weirauch)

Opposite below, right First class on the famed Strath liners – here we see the first-class main lounge on the *Straithaird*. (P&O)

P. & O. 'STRATHMORE' - 1st CLASS SPORTS DECK

The tall, raked, all-yellow funnel onboard the *Strathmore*. (P&O)

But even in the 1950s, as the North Atlantic trade began to shake with the thunderous sounds of the airplane and then the jet, the P&O-Orient Australian route seemed to have a very promising future. It led both companies, the still separately managed Orient and P&O lines, to think of the two biggest and fastest liners ever built for a service other than the North Atlantic. The Orient liner came first, the 41,900-ton *Oriana*, the fastest liner ever to sail to Australia, making the run from Southampton to Sydney via Suez in twenty-one days flat. Commissioned in December 1960, it was said that she was the first British liner that could seriously substitute for one of the 28½-knot Cunard *Queens* on the five-day Southampton-New York express run. However, and like that of the liner United States with the Blue Riband on the Atlantic, the *Oriana*'s record was the last of any consequence on a run east of Suez. While no faster passenger ships were built in fact, the appearance of aircraft on the Australian run within the next decade reduced her three-week passages to Sydney to insignificance.

P&O's new giant came several months later, the last liner in fact to come from the illustrious Harland & Wolff yards at Belfast, builders of the *Titanic* and other notable ships. Named *Canberra*, she reached 45,700 tons and could carry a maximum of 2,272 passengers (her capacity was even greater than that of the world's largest liner, the *Queen Elizabeth*, which had a full complement of 2,223 passengers). Simultaneously, the P&O-Orient Lines could advertise as having the largest as well as the fastest liners on the Australian as well as worldwide liner trades. Such distinctions as 'biggest' and 'fastest' would assure a steady flow of passengers for the two, new P&O-Orient liners. On her maiden voyage from Southampton in June 1961, the *Canberra* departed with 2,238 passengers onboard.

Architecturally as well as decoratively, P&O-Orient had shown steady improvement in their post-war liners. The public rooms grew larger and more contemporary in decor, especially aboard the *Oriana* and *Canberra*, and with such added amenities as lido bars, discos, conference rooms and, on the *Oriana*, a multi-level theatre. Far more cabins were fitted with private facilities, a strong consideration in fact for the North American passengers the Company hoped to attract by offering more and more voyages in the upper Pacific. The outdoor decks were larger than ever, with games areas, several pools and an abundance of comfortable sun and lounge chairs. By 1960, all of the post-war liners were upgraded with complete air conditioning. Onboard entertainment, which was mostly passenger inspired and created, was later expanded to include an entertainments' officer and finally a full-fledged cruise director, who produced an almost tiring schedule of all-day events – from bingo to a squash competition to a lecture on flower arranging. Like the Atlantic liner companies,

The handsome *Stratheden*, completed in 1937, finished her days as a Greek-owned Moslem pilgrim ship before being junked in Italy in 1969. (P&O)

Assisting the *Corfu* and *Carthage* on the London-Far East run was the 16,000-ton *Canton*, completed in 1939. (Richard Faber Collection)

P&O began to recognise that the liners were more than just mere transport, but they were floating hotels, sea-going resorts as well, and had to provide more and more recreation, amusement and even diversion. Many of the older, loyalist passengers, often in first-class accommodations, travelled simply for travel's sake and, even during say a 100-day trip around the world, they often remained aboard the ship while in port. P&O offered some of the world's most extensive and diverse voyages. As an example, in January 1966, the *Iberia* left London on a sixty-nine-day itinerary that took her to Gibraltar, Naples, Port Said, Aden, Bombay, Fremantle, Adelaide, Melbourne, Sydney, back to Melbourne, Fremantle and Adelaide, then Colombo, Aden, Port Said, Gibraltar and finally home to London. Fares for a full voyage began at £506 in tourist class (or $1,088 in US dollars).

The P&O passenger fleet was first affected by airline competition in the late 1960s. Responding to those initial inroads, one captain recalled, 'We sent our liners on longer and more diverse sailings, roaming the world looking for passengers to fill our increasingly empty berths'. Shortly thereafter, there were other problems as well – faster, more efficient container ships began to take passenger ship cargos, then inexpensive charter flights lured away the budget tourists and even the remaining migrant business, and finally, as the ships grew older, they needed costly refits to meet new safety, regulatory and

insurance standards. It all became painfully obvious. Like so many others, especially in the devastating 1970s, these P&O-Orient liners sailed off, like a parade of elephants, to the boneyards of Taiwan. Between 1972 and 1976, the Company retired and then scrapped the *Iberia*, *Orcades*, *Chusan*, *Himalaya*, *Orsova* and *Oronsay*. The last of the 1950s group, the *Arcadia*, went as well, but in 1979. That vast global network of passenger ship services, including many other companies similar to P&O, had come to an abrupt, quite dramatic ending. In the years ahead, it became increasingly difficult to find a one-way passage to, say, South Africa, Australia or Japan.

'Up until the 1960s, the liners still had a role to play on world trade routes and on the passenger routes, to the colonies and all across the world,' said Glasgow-based Economics Professor Tony Slaven:

These ships were really the only way of conducting business across the old sea routes. But then you had the challenge of the new generation of wider bodied, larger capacity jets. The Boeing 707 is one that really did the damage. Instead of taking thirty days to travel from London to Sydney, you could do it in thirty hours, more or less. You were very tired and you couldn't relax on the journey, but you could do it that way. I think everyone was surprised how quickly passenger preference shifted from those leisurely four-week journeys to the Antipodes by liner to one-day flights in a long, silver-coloured tube.

Above The first of the big, post-Second World War P&O-Orient liners, the 28,396-ton *Orcades* – commissioned in December 1948 – is seen here docked at San Francisco. (Richard Faber Collection)

Right Final rites – the twenty-five-year-old *Orcades* being scrapped, in a view from April 1973, at Kaohsiung on Taiwan. With the likes of the furniture, artworks, china and cutlery long since taken off, her steel structural remains were gradually despatched to the rolling mills. (James L. Shaw Collection)

The 28,000-ton *Himalaya*, completed in 1949, was the first new liner for P&O to be built following the Second World War. (Richard Faber Collection)

Above In her maiden year, in 1950, the *Chusan* – built for the London-Far East run – is seen at Tilbury, London. The veteran Orient Line passenger ship *Ormonde* is seen to the left. (P&O)

Left In her last days, the *Chusan* is seen in lay-up at Southampton, awaiting her sale to the shipbreakers, in this view dated May 1973. The *S.A. Vaal* is just to the left and the *Edinburgh Castle* further beyond. (Steffen Weirauch Collection)

Above The *Orsova* of 1954 will be novel – the first liner without a mast of any kind. Her single funnel will be her dominant external feature. She is seen here fitting-out at the Vickers-Armstrong yard at Barrow-in-Furness. (Albert Wilhelmi Collection)

Right The 27,632-ton *Oronsay* followed the *Chusan*, being launched in June 1950 and then having her maiden voyage to Australia in May 1951. (Richard Faber Collection)

ORIANA REVISITED

In the winter of 1992, when the P&O liner *Canberra* was on her annual world cruise, Ship's Photographer Ian Noble and fifteen fellow passengers set off by train from Hiroshima to the southern port of Beppu. While noted for its hot springs, Beppu was not the reason for their travels. Instead, they had a special, more specific, quite nostalgic purpose – to see the *Canberra*'s one-time running-mate, the *Oriana*. Built in 1960, that 41,900-ton ship had once been the fastest liner on the old England-Australia run. She had finished her P&O sailing days, being last used as a Sydney-based cruise ship, before being sold to Japanese interests in 1986. They wanted her for use as a hotel, museum and restaurant ship.

The 804ft-long *Oriana* had been assigned to full-time cruising from Sydney beginning in 1981.

> Her Australian cruises were very popular, often filled to the very last upper berth,' recalled a former officer. 'The Australians are, of course, well known for their high spirits, even their pranks and events that include beer-drinking contests. Consequently, we always brought along two off-duty Sydney policemen, who joined the entire cruise for added security. We'd cruise to some beautiful spots – Pago Pago and Noumea, Milford Sound and Apia. But the *Oriana* was growing old and tired by the mid-'80s. In the end, by 1986, she was actually beginning to deteriorate behind the scenes. In a good storm, A Deck might easily have become C Deck!

Rumour was that after P&O, she might become a Greek cruise ship or even be rebuilt as a large car carrier. But the Japanese bought her instead and had her towed all the way to her new island home.

'It was a typically British day when we reached Beppu Bay,' recalled Ian Noble:

> The *Oriana* was docked at the end of a long pier and appeared out of the mists and light rain. I was first struck by her pink-coloured funnels. They were no longer in the familiar P&O yellow. Otherwise, she was a very sorry sight, clearly past her best. We were piped aboard by a pair of Australian girls wearing kilts and playing the bagpipes.

While at first intended to be a hotel, the *Oriana* amassed huge losses for the Japanese. Local hotel owners protested the operation and succeeded in blocking that part of the ship's original plan. Consequently, she was little more than a poorly attended maritime museum. In the end, the losses even prompted the Daiwa Group, her real estate-rich owners, to put her back on the block. 'All of the crew areas had been closed off and some parts were actually welded shut,' added Noble:

Some public rooms had been opened out to conference areas while a few remained from her old P&O liner days. Oddly, the surgery remained, but had been relocated. It was a recreation of a ship's surgery, but in a museum setting. The engine room was also open to display, but it was very cold and damp, and therefore not at all how an engine room should be. In fact, many pieces of the original engines had been sliced away.

'The ship was quite empty,' concluded Ian Noble:

> Only a few Japanese tourists were visiting. Up on the bridge, maps and charts were still in their cupboards. There was also a plaque that commemorated all the Japanese weddings held onboard. We took a group picture on the bridge wing. Some of the 15 in our group had cruised on the ship often. To them, it was still 'the O'. They had fond memories of her.

The *Oriana*, succeeded by a 70,000-ton P&O cruise ship of the same name in 1995, was soon sold to Chinese buyers. Towed across to Chinwangtao that July, she began by being used as a Government-owned accommodation centre and hotel. Later moved to Shanghai, she seemed unsuccessful and was finally berthed in Dalian. She capsized, however, during a typhoon that struck Dalian in June 2004. Although later righted, she was beyond economic repair and so the forty-five-year-old ship was broken-up at Zhangjiagang in the spring and summer of 2005.

Opposite On an outward sailing to Australia, the 709ft-long *Oronsay* calls at the Stazione Maritima at Naples. The Dutch liner *Willem Ruys* is on the left. (Richard Faber Collection)

Above Majestic and mighty, the imposing 29,734-ton *Arcadia* departs from Sydney. (P&O)

Above During a summertime Northern Cities cruise, the *Arcadia* is seen in night-time Hamburg harbour. (Albert Wilhelmi Collection)

Opposite, left In a series of upper-deck, close-up views, here we see the funnel and bridge section of the *Orcades*. (Albert Wilhelmi Collection)

Opposite, right A view on the first-class sports deck onboard the *Iberia*. (Albert Wilhelmi Collection)

The *Iberia*, commissioned in 1954, was the first of the big P&O liners to be retired during the early 1970s. At age eighteen, she is seen departing Southampton in the summer of 1972, bound for Taiwan and the breakers. (Steffen Weirauch Collection)

Shuffleboard anyone? A sports area and the towering funnel aboard the *Oronsay*. (Albert Wilhelmi Collection)

Deck games all the way to Sydney! The so-called first-class arena onboard the 1,416-passenger *Oronsay*. (Albert Wilhelmi Collection)

Classic P&O post-war interior decor: The first-class Verandah Café onboard the *Himalaya*, 1949. (Andy Hernandez Collection)

The tourist-class dining room, also aboard the *Himalaya*. (Andy Hernandez Collection)

The best first-class suite, also known as 'the flat', aboard the *Oronsay*. (P&O)

For the final years of their London-Far East passenger run, in 1961 P&O bought two Belgian passenger-cargo ships, the *Jadotville* and *Baudouinville*, dating from 1956–57. They refitted as the *Chitral* and *Cathay* (seen here) for 240 all-first-class passengers each. Both were withdrawn by 1969–70 and sold off. (Richard Faber Collection)

P&O ARCADIA 1ST CLASS PROMENADE DECK

Above Bound for Suez: the vast first-class promenade aboard the *Arcadia*. (Albert Wilhelmi Collection)

Opposite The imposing 41,923 ton-*Oriana*, commissioned in December 1960, was the fastest liner ever to sail on the UK-Australia run, cutting the time from four to three weeks between Southampton and Sydney. Said to be the fastest British liner to be built since the *Queen Elizabeth* in 1940, the 804ft-long *Oriana* had a service speed of 27½ knots. (P&O)

The royal yacht *Britannia* is seen here astern of the *Oriana* in a view at Southampton dated August 1970. (P&O)

The 45,733-ton *Canberra*, the largest liner ever built for UK-Australian service, arrives at Southampton in November 1984 with the brand new 44,348-ton *Royal Princess* berthed to the right. (P&O)

A new life: the *Oriana* arriving at Beppu in Japan on 17 July 1986 to become a moored tourist attraction. (Yoshitatsu Fukawa)

During a cruise, the *Canberra* calls at Lisbon – with the *Pacific Princess* on the right. (Luis Miguel Correia Collection)

Farewell season: during her winter world cruise, the 818ft-long *Canberra* makes her final visit to San Francisco on 14 March 1997. (Peter Knego Collection)

Final arrival of the beloved, thirty-six-year-old *Canberra* at Southampton in September 1997. (Richard Faber Collection)

19

EXTRAORDINARY SERVICE: ROYAL MAIL LINES

The so-called Royal Mail Steam Packet Co. dated, like Cunard and several others, from the 1830s and '40s. Their interest was in the South American trades, mostly to the East Coast – to Brazil, Uruguay and Argentina. While providing a passenger link between Britain and Latin America, they profited from the great migrant trade from both Portugal and Spain, and from the meat business going northward from the Argentine.

By the 1950s, the Company was operating two large liners on the mainline service between Southampton, Lisbon, Las Palmas, Rio de Janeiro, Santos, Montevideo and Buenos Aires. The 22,100-ton *Alcantara* dated from 1926 while the handsome, 26,800-ton *Andes* was completed in September 1939, just as the Second World War began. Their first-class quarters were notable for decor as well as fine food and superb service. The *Alcantara* endured until scrapped in 1958 while the 669ft-long *Andes* was converted, in two stages, in 1959-60 as a 500-passenger, all-first-class cruise ship. Along with Cunard's *Caronia*, she became one of Britain's most luxuriously acclaimed big cruise liners. To the very end of her days, the 21-knot *Andes* had a splendid, most enviable reputation.

'She was an elegant liner made into a splendid cruise ship,' recalled Desmond Kirkpatrick, who served aboard her in the purser's department in the 1960s.

She was built from the start for a discerning clientele and this showed in her later years. She had, for example, some of the largest deck spaces afloat or so it seemed. After her conversion, she was painted all-white and looked quite handsome. She cruised mostly in warm weather waters, mostly in the Mediterranean and to the Atlantic Isles, but occasionally over to the Caribbean. I seem to recall visits to Fort Lauderdale and even New Orleans. Of course, in high summer, she might go up to Scandinavia, to the Norwegian fjords, the Baltic cities, even Iceland. She had an all-British crew. There was a tremendous number of repeat passengers including lots of aristocrats. She had fine public rooms and a main restaurant plus a grill room. For entertainment, we had lots of dancing, films, a few entertainers including local performers, lots of bridge, but nothing like today's sleek presentations. Of course, deck games during the daytime were very popular.

To supplement the East Coast of South America liner services, but from London in the 1950s (the *Alcantara* and *Andes* were based at Southampton), four motor liners, the 14,200-ton *Highland Brigade*, *Highland Princess*, *Highland Monarch* and *Highland Chieftain*, were used. Carrying some 439 passengers in first- and third-class quarters and a sizeable amount of freight, they were built in 1929–30 for the Nelson Line, which was bought out by Royal Mail in 1932. 'I had gone down to Spain and back in 1955, taking the *Highland Brigade* going down and the *Highland Monarch* coming home,' added Desmond Kirkpatrick. 'I recall the *Monarch* being so overbooked that I had to sleep in the ship's hospital for a night or two.'

These ships were replaced in 1959-60 by three, fine combination passenger-cargo ships, the 20,300-ton *Amazon*, *Aragon* and *Arlanza*, but which, in fact, proved to be Britain's last three-class liners and the last to offer third-class quarters. Their accommodations were arranged for ninety-two in first class, eighty-two in cabin class and 275 in third class. They were not, however, especially successful. By 1968–69, they were sold to the Shaw Savill Line, becoming the *Akaroa*, *Aranda* and *Arawa* respectively, but for a short-lived around-the-world passenger service. The *Aragon* closed out Royal Mail's South American passenger service with a final sailing in February 1969. By 1971, these three ships were sold again, this time to Norwegians, but to be completely rebuilt as 3,000-capacity auto carriers. All three were scrapped by 1981.

Built in 1926, the *Alcantara* was teamed after the Second World War with the *Andes* on Royal Mail's express service to South America. The 22,000-ton *Alcantara* is seen here at Cherbourg. (Albert Wilhelmi Collection)

The *Andes*, flagship of Royal Mail Lines in the 1950s and '60s, is seen while on the South American run. She is arriving at Cherbourg with the *Queen Mary* just behind and already docked. (Richard Faber Collection)

With her squat motorship stacks and in some resemblance to Cunard's *Britannic*, the *Highland Monarch* and her sisters looked after Royal Mail's South American service but from London. (Royal Mail Lines)

In her refitted style, in cruising white, the *Andes* looked much like a large yacht. (Richard Faber Collection)

Finished with engines! The *Andes*, seen here in May 1971, has just arrived at Ghent in Belgium to be scrapped. Both masts were trimmed for bridge clearance. (Steffen Weirauch Collection)

'The Three Graces' as they were called – the *Amazon*, *Aragon* (seen here) and *Arlanza* of 1959–60 were Royal Mail's final liners and the last three-class liners as well as the last ships to carry third class. (Gillespie-Faber Collection)

20

THE LAST SHAW SAVILL LINERS

Their motto was 'Ship and Travel Shaw Savill'. They were one of Britain's best known, most popular and more successful liner companies. By the late 1950s, this London-based company had two large liners and a quartet of combination passenger-cargo ships. Trading out of London as well as Southampton, their primary routes of interest were Australia and New Zealand.

A classical liner in the best tradition, their largest vessel was the 26,400-ton *Dominion Monarch*, which had been completed in 1939 by Swan, Hunter & Wigham Richardson at Newcastle. After extensive and heroic war service as a troopship, she was restored to her original, quite luxurious self. She was, in fact, a passenger ship with a very large cargo capacity. In six holds, there was space for 650,000 cubic feet of cargo. The majority of this was refrigerated, particularly for the meats that were brought home to Britain from Australia and New Zealand. Her passenger quarters were of the highest standard and might best be described as 'club like'. She carried only 508 passengers, all of them in first class. According to Scott Baty, the Sydney-based author of *Ships That Passed*, a commemorative book on bygone liners, 'The *Dominion Monarch* was considered to be the *Queen Mary* of the so-called Clipper Route – the Australian service from Britain via the South African Cape. Shaw Savill had a very good reputation at the time and the *Dominion Monarch* was their top ship.'

While distinctive as their largest passenger liner to be built on the Tyne since the Cunarder *Mauretania* in 1907, the *Dominion Monarch* was also noteworthy for her machinery. A quadruple-screw ship, she was at the time of her completion the largest motor vessel of any kind in the world. Her Doxford diesels produced 32,000 brake horsepower. Her maiden voyage out to Sydney via Capetown was expectedly something of a record-breaker. The routing from Southampton to Fremantle took just over three weeks, while the segment from Durban to Fremantle was one of the fastest runs then on record – eight days, twenty-one hours at an average speed of 19.84 knots.

Passenger ship appraiser C.M. Squarey was among the many who was evidently delighted, thrilled even, with the renowned *Dominion Monarch*. In March 1950, he wrote:

> The *Dominion Monarch* – the very name is stirring and becomes well this ship of sturdy worth, not, perhaps, the prettiest ship afloat, but certainly rich in charm and indisputable good taste. I went round in this ship from London (where she loaded her cargo) to Southampton (where she took on her passengers) with just one of the Company managers and myself onboard, watching those concerned satisfying themselves as she was 'perfectly preened' for her embarkation at Southampton; it gave me an unhustled and exceedingly pleasant opportunity to spot and appreciate her many virtues.

Peter Buttfield, an Australian who had spent nearly fifty years in shoreside passenger ship operations, also recalled the *Dominion Monarch*:

> I remember her from that fateful summer of 1939. When war in Europe was about to be declared, the *Monarch* – as we called her – had been especially loaded with much-needed produce from Australia and New Zealand. It had even been placed in crates in the lounges. The British Government was especially reluctant to convert her for transport duty because she was so luxurious. Once in military service, however, she remained a regular visitor to Australian waters, mostly with troops and, later, with war brides.

The *Dominion Monarch* was, however, no longer the best economic blend of passenger and cargo carrier by the late '50s. With the blazing success of the then new *Southern Cross*, added by Shaw Savill in 1955 and boasting all-passenger as well as all-tourist-class designs, the

Actually a big combination passenger-cargo ship, the good-looking *Dominion Monarch* was always thought of, however, as a liner. She is seen departing from London on her maiden voyage in February 1939. (Cronican-Arroyo Collection)

Commissioned in April 1947, the 15,682-ton, eighty-five-passenger *Corinthic* was the first of four combo liners built for Shaw Savill's London-Panama-New Zealand service. (Richard Faber Collection)

older ship was no longer compatible. Shaw Savill sold the *Dominion Monarch* to a Japanese scrapyard in February 1962, assuming that she would go directly to the breaker's yard. Instead, she was leased for some months for use as a hotel ship at the 1962 World's Fair in Seattle. Once this task ended, in November of that year, she crossed to Osaka, as the *Dominion Monarch Maru*, and was then broken-up.

Just after the Second World War, Shaw Savill had decided to continue the 'club-like' stylings of the *Dominion Monarch*, but in much smaller ships with far less accommodation. Four combination passenger-cargo liners, to be called *Corinthic*, *Athenic*, *Gothic* and *Ceramic*, with space for eighty-five first-class passengers only, were ordered. The *Corinthic*, the first of the quartet, was launched in May 1946 and was commissioned eleven months later. According to Scott Baty, 'These ships were a follow-up to the *Dominion Monarch* and aimed at the upper middle class market.'

These 15,000-ton ships plied a different service, however – from London out to Curacao and the Panama Canal, and then onwards to Auckland, Wellington and other ports in New Zealand. Peter Buttfield recalled their long-haul services.

They were good little ships, but difficult to 'turn around' with offloading and reloading. Often, they would spend eight to ten weeks in New Zealand, loading meat and other freezer cargos. They would arrive at Wellington and then often go to Lyttleton, Port Chalmers and occasionally back to Wellington and then to Auckland. Actually, the advertised, posted schedules were very difficult to keep. Also, during these long port stays, we would run tours over these ships for travel agents and perspective passengers. They were marketed to travellers who wanted 'business class' atmosphere. You might say that they were the ideal cabin or second class-type ships. Comparatively, in the late 1940s, it was £109 to the UK.

The first two ships, the *Corinthic* and *Athenic*, were noticeably different from the second pair. Among other features, they had smaller and shorter funnels. The *Gothic* remains the best remembered, of course. She was selected to serve as a Royal Yacht, in 1953–54, for Her Majesty Queen Elizabeth II's Commonwealth Tour. I recall seeing her at the time, having been especially repainted with an all-white hull. She was given wonderful receptions wherever she appeared.

This foursome remained in passenger service for nearly twenty years. The *Athenic* and *Corinthic*, by then struggling with airline competitors and stricter evaluations from Home Office accountants, were reduced to full-time freighters by 1965. Three years later, both were broken-up in Taiwan. Also, in the late '60s, both the *Gothic* and *Corinthic* were downgraded to freighters. The *Ceramic* survived the longest of all, going to Belgian shipbreakers in 1972. The *Gothic* had a far less gentle ending, however. On 2 August 1968, when some 800 miles from Wellington, she caught fire. Some of those aboard were killed. Badly damaged, she finally reached New Zealand, but where full repairs were found to be

Specially chartered by the British Government, the *Gothic* is seen taking on supplies and some cargo in the London Docks in a view dated 11 November 1953. She would later sail to Kingston, Jamaica, where Queen Elizabeth II and the Duke of Edinburgh would join the 560ft-long ship for an extended Commonwealth Tour. While serving as a temporary royal yacht, the *Gothic* was especially repainted in white. (Cronican-Arroyo Collection)

uneconomic, especially in view of her age. After one final trip out to Australia (on loan to another British shipowner, the Cairn Line), she too went to Taiwanese breakers. She reached Kaohsiung in August 1969.

'Dramatically and quite suddenly, Shaw Savill decided upon a completely new image in the early 1950s,' said Scott Baty.

> They changed from the upper-market tone of the *Dominion Monarch* and the *Corinthic* class, and instead decided to seek 'youth and migrant' passengers. They wanted the budget European tourists and the new settlers on the outbound trips to Australia as well as the Australian 'backpackers' and disgruntled settlers on the homeward sailings. Thus came the age of the *Southern Cross*, which was named by Her Majesty the Queen at the Harland & Wolff yard at Belfast on 17 August 1954. She was a revolutionary ship, completely novel, different and newsworthy, much the same as the P&O *Royal Princess* was to cruise ships in the mid-'80s. The *Southern Cross* – which was always known to her crew as the 'Suffering Cross', because of somewhat less than idyllic onboard working conditions – was the first major liner to have her funnel placed aft, carry no commercial cargo whatsoever and offer comfortable, but low-fare, all-tourist class quarters for 1,100 passengers. Appropriately, she was placed on a seventy-six-day schedule that went completely around the world [from Southampton to Las Palmas, Capetown, Durban, Fremantle, Melbourne, Sydney, Auckland, Wellington, Suva, Papeete, the Panama Canal, Curacao, Trinidad and then home to Southampton]. She was a huge success at the time, but Shaw Savill's image was never again the same.

Pleased and encouraged with the success of the 20,200-ton *Southern Cross*, Shaw Savill ordered, in 1960, an even larger version, the 24,700-ton, 1,437-passenger *Northern Star*. She was named by Her Majesty Queen Elizabeth the Queen Mother at the Vickers Armstrong yard at Newcastle on 27 June 1961, and then commissioned a year later, in July 1962. At the time, however, she attracted far less attention than her predecessor and was, in fact, far less than an overall success. According to Scott Baty:

> She was designed purposely to cash-in on the £10 fare-assisted migrant trade out to Australia and as Shaw Savill's response to the rival P&O-Orient's very ambitious, far larger team, the brand new *Oriana* and *Canberra*. But the *Northern Star* was literally 'flung together' for quick profits. She was all formica and lino, and always seemed to have a list. The *Southern Cross* was the better of the two and had more quality, such as veneers in the passenger accommodation. Also, the Company always seemed to be experimenting with the *Northern Star*. I recall that they even changed her funnel colours and a put a Detroit-style automobile grill on her stack. It looked like something from a Cadillac. I suppose that she might have been converted, at least in later years, to the ideal cruise ship, but then her engines were faulty as well. Clearly, she was a mistake from day one.

In the late '60s, with ships such as the *Dominion Monarch* long gone and the *Corinthic* class retired as well, Shaw Savill – with the *Southern Cross* and *Northern Star* – hoped to strengthen their Australia-New Zealand passenger trades. These were clearly fading at the time, however, due to increased airline competition. The Company also wanted a larger share of both the UK and Australian cruise businesses, even if both of these had very definite limitations. It seems, at least in retrospect, to have been misguided times for the Company. The future direction of liner operations was divided as well as unclear. In fact, these years were to be the last ones for Shaw Savill's passenger ship operations.

In 1968, the Furness Withy Group, owners of Shaw Savill as well as Royal Mail Lines, decided to transfer Royal Mail's three 20,300-ton combination ships, the *Amazon*, *Aragon* and *Arlanza*, over to Shaw Savill. They became the *Akaroa*, *Aranda* and *Arawa* respectively. Restyled with 470 one-class berths (they had been three-class ships) and with their sizeable cargo capacities in tact, they were routed mostly on around-the-world sailings – from London to the Azores, Barbados, Trinidad, Curacao, the Panama Canal, Tahiti, Auckland, Wellington, Sydney, Melbourne, Fremantle, Durban, Capetown and Las Palmas before returning to the UK. Most unfortunately, they could not have been less successful. According to Scott Baty, 'Shaw Savill wanted to return to something of the *Corinthic* class-type of service with these three ships, which were known as the "White Herons". Simply, it was too late for that type of passenger-cargo ship. The era of the combination liner had passed for the most part.'

The *Akaroa*, *Aranda* and *Arawa* were sold, after little more than two years in Shaw Savill service, in 1971. They went to Norwegian buyers, but not for further passenger services. Instead, in a rather novel fate for out-of-work passenger ships, they were converted, with great structural alterations, to car carriers, each with a capacity for as many as 3,000 autos. Renamed *Akarita*, *Hoegh Traveller* and *Hoegh Transit* respectively (and with several name and ownership changes to follow), they ran on worldwide services until broken-up in Taiwan in 1981.

Shortly after Shaw Savill acquired the three former Royal Mail sisters, the Company had ambitious ideas about strengthening its 'big liner' cruise ship services. In February 1970, they bought Canadian Pacific's 25,000-ton *Empress of England*, a former transatlantic liner that had been built by Vickers-Armstrong at Newcastle in 1957. Renamed *Ocean Monarch*, she was briefly used in Australian service, but was then taken in hand for an extensive, but troublesome, often-delayed refit. She remained at a Birkenhead shipyard for over a year, from September 1970. With increased cruising-only accommodations for 1,372 passengers (it had been 1,058), she was used in both British and Australian cruise service. Shaw Savill had even hoped to supplement

Finishing touches! The brand new *Southern Cross* being handled by tugs at the Harland & Wolff yard at Belfast. It is early 1955 and soon the all-tourist-class ship will be off on a year of sold-out voyages, three trips around the world and three short cruises. (Cronican-Arroyo Collection)

The Tavern was one of the most popular public areas aboard the 1,100-passenger *Southern Cross*. (Shaw Savill Line)

The forward dining room. (Shaw Savill Line)

The forward foyer adjacent to the lounge. (Shaw Savill Line)

this further by acquiring another Canadian Pacific liner, the *Empress of Canada*, which would have become the *Dominion Monarch*. This latter plan never materialised, however.

Amidst the difficulties and delays with the *Ocean Monarch*, Shaw Savill's UK cruising program – mostly from Southampton, but occasionally from Liverpool as well – was less than encouraging and consequently, in March 1971, the *Southern Cross* was abruptly withdrawn from service. Laid-up for a time at Southampton, she was later moved to the River Fal in Cornwall, an increasingly crowded anchorage for money-losing, out-of-work British passenger ships. Amidst rumours that she might become a floating youth hostel, she was sold instead, in March 1973, to the Greek-flag Ulysses Line for conversion into the cruise ship *Calypso*. She later sailed as the *Azure Seas* and then the *Ocean Breeze*, before being scrapped in Pakistan in 2003.

By the 1972 cruise season, Shaw Savill had dropped from six to two liners. Only the *Northern Star* and *Ocean Monarch* remained. The Company's once impeccable image was no longer quite the same. Scott Baty recalled the disappointment with the converted *Ocean Monarch*.

> During her long refit, the Company spent all of the money on decor and none of it on the engines. They were in very poor condition by the early '70s. Consequently, she was always breaking down, was always days late and once almost had to be towed home from a cruise. Once, I recall seeing her at Auckland, looking rusty and dreadful. Her days were clearly numbered.

John Smythe, a cruise director with Shaw Savill in the early '70s, recalled those final years as well.

> The *Southern Cross*, the elder of the three remaining liners, still had a certain distinctiveness about her, a certain reputation, even in the very end. There was still a certain social status about cruising in her, even if it was cheap. The *Northern Star* had fantastic atmosphere for cruising. We carried a staff of sixteen professional entertainers onboard. But unfortunately, the boilers were always breaking down. Adequate time was never taken for proper repairs. The *Ocean Monarch* was the most unfortunate of all, however. She was a disaster from the very start. She too was always breaking down, but also, because the British unions never liked her, there was industrial sabotage onboard. There were lots of broken toilets, for example.

The *Northern Star*'s troubles included an engine room explosion off Venice during a Mediterranean cruise in June 1974, and this was complicated further by several headline-making, unsatisfactory health inspections. Then, problems for both ships were more than doubled when fuel oil prices drastically increased in 1973–74.

The *Ocean Monarch* was withdrawn first and, following a brief lay-up at Southampton, was delivered to Taiwanese breakers in the summer of 1975. The *Northern Star*, now the last Shaw Savill liner, lasted until October 1975 and then she too went to the Taiwanese. She was dismantled the following spring. Stephen Card, a former officer with Shaw Savill and today a very distinguished maritime artist, added, 'On that last, otherwise empty sailing out to Kaohsiung, the *Northern Star* carried a complement of cadets. They were kept busy until the very end of the trip, clipping and then repainting the otherwise scrap-bound ship.'

Shaw Savill briefly continued in cruise service, but in Australia as Shaw Savill Holidays, using the chartered Soviet liner *Feodor Shalyapin*, the former Cunarder *Franconia*. However, according to John Smythe, 'After ten months, the Soviets would not renew the charter for the ship. They realised the potential success and so had their cruise subsidiary, the CTC Lines, take over.' Shaw Savill, by then a dwindling cargo ship owner, was now out of the passenger trades entirely.

Right Having become the Greek *Calypso* and then the *Azure Seas*, the former *Southern Cross* spent her final years as the *Ocean Breeze*. She is seen here arriving at Key West, Florida, on 5 December 1996. (Clive Harvey Collection)

The 24,731-ton *Northern Star*, commissioned in July 1962, was an enlarged version of the highly successful *Southern Cross*. Unfortunately, the new ship was less than an overall success and was withdrawn and then scrapped at the age of fourteen. (Luis Miguel Correia Collection)

The *Ocean Monarch*, the former *Empress of England*, is seen here at Auckland. (Luis Miguel Correia Collection)

In 1968–69, Shaw Savill took over the South American combo liners *Amazon*, *Aragon* and *Arlanza* and renamed respectively as *Akaroa*, *Aranda* (seen in this view) and *Arawa* for around-the-world voyages. (Luis Miguel Correia Collection)

Almost unrecognisable, the former *Aranda* (ex-*Aragon*) is seen here, passing through the Suez Canal, as the 3,000-car capacity *Hoegh Trotter*. In the end, she went to Taiwanese breakers in 1981. (James L. Shaw Collection)

OUT OF AFRICA: UNION-CASTLE LINE

It has been some thirty years since the Union-Castle/Safmarine passenger service to the South African Cape was closed out. It was then one of the very last major liner routes, British-flag or otherwise, still surviving. It was a trade that included some very beautiful, very handsome ships. John Dimmock joined Union-Castle in February 1949, when the Company had no less than nineteen liners. Decades later, in July 1985, we met aboard Safmarine Lines' *Astor*, where he served as purser. He recalled his earlier years:

My first assignment at Union-Castle was the *Pretoria Castle* [28,700 tons], then brand new [commissioned in July 1948] and on Voyage Number 6, on the Cape Mail Express route between Southampton, Las Palmas, Capetown, Port Elizabeth, East London and Durban. She and her sister, the *Edinburgh Castle*, were then the very best liners in the fleet and everyone, or so it seemed, wanted to travel in them. Passengers nearly queued-up for passages. Carrying 214 in first class and 541 in tourist class, the last-named quarters were then used mostly by migrants. The South African Government paid £100 toward the migrant fares for selected professionals, namely engineers, scientists and teachers. It was not quite the huge migrant scheme run by the Australian Government, but the South Africans undertook a sizeable recruitment in those immediate post-war years.

Union-Castle was the ideal 'career company' in those times, the future looked tremendous and one could expect to reach full purser's rank by their late forties or fifties. In those early years, as the lowest member of the purser's department, you had non-officer status and were not allowed on the passenger decks. We were allowed, however, two bottles of beer each day!

The Union-Castle passenger fleet was quite diverse in the late 1940s and included not only the big mailships on the Cape run, but smaller and older ships that worked the so-called intermediate trades. John Dimmock served in these ships as well and later on the Company's extensive Round Africa run.

I was assigned to the *Durban Castle*, a 17,000-tonner, built in 1938 and normally on our Round Africa service, but which was temporarily assigned to the fast mail service to the Cape while some of our other, large liners were still undergoing their post-war restorations. The 18-knot *Durban Castle* took a day longer than the larger ships [fifteen days], but was otherwise an ideal substitute. She had very comfortable accommodations for 180 first class and 359 in tourist class. At the time, long before the tourist boom, we still carried mostly port-to-port passengers. While we carried a dance band, the remaining entertainment was arranged and organised by a passenger sports & entertainment committee. There was heavy emphasis on deck games during the day and, for evenings, there was dog-racing, the so-called 'Ocean Derby', fancy dress, a talent show and quizzes. Ironically, passengers were not allowed to dance in the public rooms in those years as we had a very religious company chairman at the time. Instead, they would dance along the promenade deck.

John Dimmock was next posted to the *Arundel Castle*, a one-time four-stacker that had been rebuilt and modernised with only two funnels in the late 1930s. She had been built originally in 1921.

This grand old ship was retained by the British Government for some years after the War. We sailed mostly to and from Port Said via Gibraltar and Malta with troops and Government-related passengers. The original first class was used by military officers, who had metal beds. The old second and third class sections had been made into huge dormitories for the troops. Mostly, we carried Royal Air Force and Royal Navy personnel.

The little *Llanstephan Castle* [11,293 tons] sailed out of London on our Round Africa service, which included calls at – in the 'out west' direction – at Las Palmas, Ascension, St Helena, Capetown, Port Elizabeth, East London, Durban, Lourenco Marques, Beira, Dar-es-Salaam, Zanzibar, Tanga, Mombasa, Aden, Port Sudan, Suez, Port Said, Genoa, Marseilles and Gibraltar. I especially remember that the best cabin onboard, with private bath and toilet, cost £100 for the 3½ weeks

A classic liner: the *Arundel Castle*, built in 1922, originally had four funnels, but was modernised with two in 1937. (Richard Faber Collection)

from London to Capetown. In those years, we carried lots of British civil servants, 'crown agents people' as they were also called, and mostly to and from what was then colonial East Africa. There wasn't any air conditioning in such elderly ships and instead we relied on the old punkah forced air ventilation system. Fortunately, and particularly in the first class section, there were lots of outside cabins or rooms that had at least some form of open-air exposure. In the holds, we carried general cargo southbound and then brought large amounts of copper and coffee on the homeward runs. In those often sweltering African ports, we had to use good sense and allow the crew to work at their own pace. It seemed that most tasks were done over longer periods. When we returned after those three-month roundtrips, we had three weeks in the London Docks. That period was considered shore leave and then you returned in time for the next sailing.

Dimmock was later assigned to the 18,400-ton *Bloemfontein Castle*, built in 1950 and unique within the Union-Castle fleet in that she carried only one-class of passengers, 721 all-cabin class.

This ship was built especially for the outward migrant trade that was inspired by the South & East African groundnut scheme. There was to have been a huge flow of British workers and their families, but unfortunately it all never materialised. Consequently, this ship was the 'odd duckling' in our fleet. She was placed instead on a special East African intermediate service, rounding the Cape and then going as far as Beira. She was, of course, an interesting experiment for Union-Castle with her one-class quarters. Her passengers did, however, tend to grade themselves – selecting their own type and style of public rooms. Some wanted the luxury bars

and others the spit'n sawdust style. In addition to the British passengers, we also carried Dutch, Germans and Portuguese as well, and often taking the overflow from other ships. In those years, in the early 1950s, there was still only one plane a week to South & East Africa.

The most interesting and exciting adventure aboard the *Bloemfontein Castle* was her heroic rescue of the passengers and crew from the *Klipfontein*, a passenger-cargo ship from the Holland-Africa Line, on 8 January 1953. We had just been together at Lourenco Marques and we were both racing for the single dock at Beira. Unfortunately, the *Klipfontein* ran aground and then began to break in half and finally sank. We received an SOS just after lunch and got to the stricken vessel by late afternoon. We managed to save everyone and everything including a Dachshund and a canary.

John Dimmock rose continuously within the ranks of the Union-Castle passenger fleet. As an assistant purser, he served on the Round Africa service and then went to the more prestigious Cape Mail run. Later, when promoted to second purser, it was back to the Round Africa ships and then later back to the Mail run. It was a set procedure in those years.

I was made full purser for the maiden voyage of our brand new *Transvaal Castle*, a 32,600-tonner completed early in 1962. She was then our experimental 'hotel ship' with 728 total berths, all in the equivalent of cabin or second class and with a range of accommodation from top-deck suites to economical, family-style four-berth rooms.

John later served for thirteen years as chief purser on the Company's flagship and largest liner, the 37,600-ton *Windsor Castle*. Expectedly, he had special memories of what would become the final years of the famed Cape Mail Express.

The *Windsor Castle* [completed in 1960] and the 28,500-ton *Pendennis Castle* [1958] were our most favoured big ships and we had regular passengers who came year after year. It was often much like a large, sea-going club. I especially remember one sailing on the *Windsor Castle* wherein every first class passenger was titled. Of course, they all knew one another from previous trips and entered completely into the spirit of the voyage. These passengers would, like so many others, catch the first sailing after New Years and would transfer, or so it seemed, from the first class lounge on the *Windsor* or *Pendennis* to the main lounge of the Mount Nelson Hotel in Capetown, which was, by the way, also owned by Union-Castle. Most of them, having escaped the dreary British winter and were therefore rather affectionately known as 'winter dodgers', would then return on a northbound sailing in April or May. Each year, we would rotate the first outward sailing in January between the *Windsor Castle* and the *Pendennis Castle*.

While we had six other large liners on the Cape route [*Athlone Castle*, *Stirling Castle*, *Capetown Castle*, *Edinburgh Castle*, *Pretoria Castle* and *Transvaal Castle*],

Veteran passenger ships from the 1920s: the *Llangibby Castle* was used into the 1950s on the London-Round Africa service. (Richard Faber Collection)

When completed in 1936, the 25,500-ton sisters *Stirling Castle* (seen here departing from Capetown) and *Athlone Castle* were the large Union-Castle liners on the mailship run to Capetown. (Robert Pabst Collection)

Originally built with two squat funnels, the *Winchester Castle* of 1930 was rebuilt eight years later with a more traditional, flat, wide Union-Castle funnel. (Richard Faber Collection)

the Cayzer family, which owned Union-Castle, and in particular Mr Nicholas Cayzer, thought of the *Windsor Castle* and *Pendennis Castle* as floating clubs in first class. They were decorated with specially woven carpets and objects d'art. Mr Cayzer would always visit these two ships at Southampton and, with a naval architect in tow, always look to improve and alter their first class accommodations. Everything always had to be in perfect condition, which, of course, justified those first class fares [£412 for a roundtrip sailing to the Cape in 1961].

In 1965, Union-Castle accelerated its mailship services and reduced its Cape-bound fleet to five liners and two high-speed freighters.

The cargo liners, the *Good Hope Castle* and *Southampton Castle*, were known as the 'mini mails' and were later fitted with twelve passenger berths, an alteration underwritten by the British Government, as the ships called also at remote St Helena. Their visits, with passengers, cargo and mail, were among the very few links with Britain.

As we advanced the mailship run, increasing the schedules from six and a half to seven and a half voyages per year for each ship, which was a large economy move, we also noted changing trends in our passenger trading. There were certainly more and more tourists travelling with us. Our peak sailings were between January and March on the southbound trips and between April and June on the northbound runs. The rest of the year, we began going lighter and lighter. Of course, cargo was still an important aspect of our economics on these passenger liners, particularly

the fruits, wools, hides, gold and bulk wine from South Africa. Of course, the mail remained especially important in both directions. Ironically, it was that very cargo that would spark the demise of the Union-Castle liners.

The South African Marine Corporation, the Safmarine Lines, took on shared management in 1966 of the *Pretoria Castle*, which was renamed *S.A. Oranje*, and the new *Transvaal Castle*, which changed to *S.A. Vaal*. By 1969, the two ships changed to South African registry as well.

By the mid-1970s, the Union-Castle liner runs were losing money. While all of the pre-war liners had been retired and even with the joint effort with Safmarine Lines, further decline was ahead. In 1975–76, the older *Edinburgh Castle* and *S.A. Oranje*, the former *Pretoria Castle*, were retired and sold off to Far Eastern shipbreakers. Soon afterward, the newer, eighteen-year-old *Pendennis Castle* was sold to Hong Kong buyers. By 1977, only two liners – the *Windsor Castle* and the *S.A. Vaal* (ex-*Transvaal Castle*) – remained and sailed within a revised fleet of mostly large, high-speed containerships. Later that year, in October, the passenger runs ended completely. John Dimmock well remembered this historic closing:

There had been a rumour that the passenger mail service would continue after 1977, but the Safmarine Lines, our increasingly stronger partner, vetoed this and

The 20,148-ton, 1926-built *Carnarvon Castle* is seen here just after the Second World War, in 1947–49, when she sailed as an immigrant ship to South Africa. She was later refitted and restored for further commercial service. (Alex Duncan)

The sisters *Durban Castle* and *Warwick Castle*, completed in 1938–39, were smaller, slower and created especially for the long, port-intensive Round Africa service. (Richard Faber Collection)

Post-war sensations! When completed in 1948, the sisters *Pretoria Castle* (shown here) and *Edinburgh Castle* were the largest and finest Castle liners to date. (Albert Wilhelmi Collection)

decided instead to build more large containerships. Quite simply, containers were the future and not passengers. Even the Cayzer family had lost interest and so the Union-Castle liner runs were ended.

The *Windsor Castle* was sold off to the Greek-owned Latsis Line to become the *Margarita L*, a workers' accommodation ship moored in Saudi Arabia, and then scrapped in India in 2005 after a long lay-up. The *S.A. Vaal* went to then new Carnival Cruise Lines of Miami and was rebuilt as the cruise ship *Festivale*. She became the *Island Breeze* for Dolphin Cruise Lines in 1996 and then changed to *Big Red Boat III* for Premier Cruise Lines in 2000. Laid up in late 2000 following the collapse of Premier, she too was broken-up out in India, but in 2003, two years before the former *Windsor Castle*. These ships were by then the last direct links to Union-Castle.

'I had spent the final thirteen years as purser in the *Windsor Castle*,' said Dimmock. 'I knew most of the regular passengers and most of them knew me. There was an important sense of permanency, continuity. The final voyage wasn't a sell-out, but to some loyal and nostalgic passengers, the question was raised: "How will we get to South Africa in the future?"'

John Dimmock went ashore for a time, like so many former Union-Castle personnel, and where he managed a leisure centre. Later, he became a part owner of a 1,000-ton coastal freighter, which sailed mostly in the North and Irish seas. 'I worked onboard as a cook,' he concluded, 'just to keep an eye on things and on the seven other crewmembers.'

John actually returned to passenger shipping, becoming purser on the little passenger-cargo ship *St Helena*, then the chartered *Centaur* and *World Renaissance*, and, in 1984–85, on Safmarine Lines' *Astor*. It was Safmarine's short-lived ambition to reopen the Capetown-Southampton. While the *Astor* venture was short-lived, a new *St Helena*, completed in 1989, sails currently, but from Capetown only.

Above The 747ft-long *Pretoria Castle* was transferred over to the management of the Safmarine Lines in 1966 and, repainted in their colours, was renamed *S.A. Oranje*. Three years later, she changed to the South African flag. (Richard Faber Collection)

Left Three 17,000-tonners were built for the Round Africa service in 1951–52. Carrying some 550 all-cabin-class passengers each, they were the *Rhodesia Castle*, *Kenya Castle* (shown here) and *Braemar Castle*. The *Kenya Castle* had the longest career, later becoming the Greek cruise ship *Amerikanis*. (Robert Pabst Collection)

Above The 18,400-ton *Bloemfontein Castle*, completed in 1950, was rather unique in the Union-Castle fleet: she carried only one class of passengers. Used on extended South and East African service, she was unsuccessful and sold within nine years to the Greeks, becoming the *Patris* of Chandris Lines. (Richard Faber Collection)

Right The first of a new generation of Castle liners, the 28,582-ton *Pendennis Castle*, commissioned in January 1959, were yet faster ships. She was designed to cut the Southampton-Capetown passage from thirteen to eleven and a half days. (Robert Pabst Collection)

The largest Castle liner of all, the 37,640-ton *Windsor Castle* was launched by Queen Elizabeth the Queen Mother in June 1959 and commissioned in August 1960. (Union-Castle Line)

The last Castle mailship was the 32,697-ton *Transvaal Castle*, added to the fleet in January 1961. She had an added notation – her 763 passengers were all carried in so-called 'hotel class'. The veteran *Capetown Castle*, dating from 1938, is berthed to the left. (Union-Castle Line)

A section of the main restaurant aboard the *Transvaal Castle*. (Union-Castle Line)

Transferred to Safmarine Lines' management in 1966 and renamed *S.A. Vaal*, the Clydebank-built ship switched to South African registry in 1969. She made the final Union-Castle/Safmarine passenger sailing in September 1977. (Richard Faber Collection)

End of her days – the laid-up *Red Boat III*, the former *S.A. Vaal* and with the idle *Rembrandt*, ex-*Rotterdam*, alongside at Freeport, Grand Bahamas, in 2001. Two years later, the former Castle liner was towed to India and broken-up. (Richard Faber Collection)

Photographed in December 1998, the lido deck aboard the *Margarita L*, the former *Windsor Castle*, is in a neglected state. The ship, laid up in Greece from 1991 for fourteen years, was towed to India and scrapped. By then, in 2005, she was the very last Union-Castle liner. (Peter Knego Collection)

Fitting conclusion! A British ocean liner favourite: the cruise ship *Reina Del Mar* sailed for Union-Castle from 1964 until scrapped in 1975–76. Her one-class, leisure, fun-in-the-sun voyages has led to today's booming British cruise industry and to far larger British cruise ships. (Richard Faber Collection)

AFTERWORD

Absolutely nostalgic and indeed part of a romantic past, most of the passenger lines and all the ships mentioned in these pages are no more. This is meant to be something of a reminder of the final golden age of British passenger shipping. But there is great, most encouraging continuity. When Cunard's 67,000-ton *Queen Elizabeth II* was commissioned in 1969, many thought that she would be the last Atlantic liner and, beyond, possibly the last British passenger liner. But these days, in 2007, the British passenger ship business is nothing short of booming. Alone, one million cruise passengers sail from UK ports. And so, a new generation of British liners sail and prosper. Cunard, 168 years old in 2007, now has three *Queens* – the *QE2*, in fact, made her celebratory fortieth anniversary cruise in September 2007; the 151,000-ton *Queen Mary II*, commissioned in 2004 and the largest Atlantic liner ever; and the 90,000-ton *Queen Victoria*, completed in December 2007.

Meanwhile, P&O's passenger division is bigger than ever. The 116,000-ton, 3,114-berth *Ventura*, commissioned in April 2008, and an unnamed sister for 2009 are the largest P&O liners yet. Then there's the 82,000-ton *Arcadia*, the 77,000-ton *Oceana*, the 76,000-ton *Aurora*, the 69,000-ton *Oriana* and the 44,000-ton *Artemis*. Also, a P&O arm, there's the Ocean Village division with the 63,000-ton *Ocean Village* and the 70,000-ton *Ocean Village Two*. Saga Cruises has two veteran, but very popular liners: the 24,000-ton *Saga Rose*, ex-*Sagafjord* of 1965, and the 24,000-ton *Saga Ruby*, the former *Vistafjord* dating from 1973. They also run the smaller, 9,500-ton *Spirit of Adventure*. Voyages of Discovery operates another veteran, the 20,000-ton *Discovery*, the former *Island Venture*, dating from 1972. And so, rest assured, there is further growth for British passenger ships, more data to be compiled and clearly further books to be written about them.

BIBLIOGRAPHY

Crowdy, Michael & O'Donoghue, Kevin (editors). *Marine News*. Kendal, Cumbria: World Ship Society, 1964-2007.

Devol, George & Cassidy, Thomas (editors). *Ocean & Cruise News*. Stamford, Connecticut: World Ocean & Cruise Society, 1980-2007.

Dunn, Laurence. *Passenger Liners*. Southampton: Adlard Coles Ltd, 1961.

—. *Passenger Liners* (revised edition). Southampton; Adlard Coles Ltd, 1965.

Eisele, Peter & Rau, William (editors). *Steamboat Bill*. Providence, Rhode Island: Steamship Historical Society of America Inc, 1964-2007.

Kludas, Arnold & Heine, Frank & Lose, Frank. *Die Grossen Passagier-schiffe der Welt.* Hamburg: Koehlers Verlagsgesellschaft, 2006.

Haws, Duncan. *Merchant Fleets: Cunard Line*. Hereford, England: TCL Publications, 1987.

Mayes, William. *Cruise Ships.* Windsor, England: Overview Press Ltd, 2005.

Miller, William H. *British Ocean Liners: A Twilight Era 1960-85.* New York: W.W. Norton & Co, 1986.

—, *Pictorial Encyclopedia of Ocean Liners, 1864-1994.* Mineola, New York: Dover Publications Inc, 1995.

—, *Picture History of British Ocean Liners.* Mineola, New York: Dover Publications Inc, 2001.

—, *Picture History of the Cunard Line 1840-1990.* Mineola, New York: Dover Publications Inc, 1991.

—, *Transatlantic Liners 1945-1980.* Newton Abbot, Devon: David & Charles Ltd, 1981.